MORETON & DISTRICTS PATRIOTS 1914-1919

S McGreal

by Stephen McGreal

Stephen McGreal was born in 1954. He is a self-employed rocking horse maker and restorer. For most of his life he has been a keen student of military history, specialising in the Great War. His knowledge has frequently reunited estranged families with biographical details revealing the final resting place of fallen soldier relations.

He is also a voluntary military researcher for a local radio station, helping to resolve listeners' military queries off-air. He is also a regular contributor to authors researching local military books.

In 1996 the author made his first pilgrimmage to France and Belgium, where he extensively toured the cemeteries, monuments and battlefields. Totally moved by the entire experience he resolved to complete a discarded research project, which has evolved to become this book.

First published 1999 by Countyvise Limited, 14 Appin Road, Birkenhead, Merseyside, CH41 9HH in conjunction with the author Stephen McGreal.

British Library Cataloguing in Publication Data.
A Catalogue record for this book is available from the British Library.

ISBN 1 901231 15 1

This book is dedicated to the memory of my
Grandfather **Private John Joseph McGreal,**
a Soldier of the Great War who served with the Cheshire
Regiment and the Machine Gun Corps, for the duration
of the Great War.

Also

My Great Grandfather **John Philip Meehan**, a seaman
with the Mercantile Marine, who survived the
torpedoing of the S.S. Persic in 1918.

Contents

INTRODUCTION

As we dash about our daily duties few passers by give the Pasture Road War Memorial a second glance, hardly any one spends a thoughtful minute contemplating the fate of the gallant men whose names are engraved with pride upon the Memorials brass plaques. Decades after their inscription the surnames are still familiar, as most still have direct descendants residing in the now busy, ever expanding town of Moreton.

Annually the memorial is the scene of a short pilgrimage, led by a dwindling band of dignified ex servicemen and women, whose chests proudly display rows of medals which glint in the weak November sun. Most of these veterans are survivors of a war fought over a half century ago, or a recent yet just as deadly conflict in the Falklands, Gulf, Bosnia or the dimly lit streets of Belfast. While the memorial now commemorates the dead of all wars, it was originally erected to honour the fallen of the Great War, an all consuming conflict which raged over eighty years ago.

Originally the surnames of the fallen Great War servicemen were synonymous with strange foreign place names such as Ypres, Lys, Bellewaarde to name just a few. These infamous battles which played their part in annihilating a generation, were once common household words, which have now been forgotten obscured by the mists of time. If the every day populace can no longer remember or perhaps more accurately care about these battles which terminated or maimed young men, what is remembered of the individual soldier? Of the legions of men who marched away many would not survive or would return shattered in mind or limb. In most instances the young fallen soldier remains an enigma, remembered vaguely as Dad's or Grandfathers brother who was killed somewhere on the Somme.

As a keen amateur military historian, having often pondered on the fates of the "Moreton Patriots" my curiosity led to enquiries regarding their untimely demise. The initial enquiries led to a

1

search for casualty headstones within the confines of the nearby church yard of Christ Church, Moreton. The inscriptions on some of the headstones revealed the fates of several of the Moreton soldiers, while others gave details of men not listed on the War Memorial. Both of these groups have been included in this tribute, despite some of the latter group having only tenuous Moreton connections.

As the vast majority of First World War veterans are no longer with us, their personal memories have now passed to history, my research had now come to an abrupt halt. The sage of Chelsea, Thomas Carlyle stated "All mankind has done, thought, gained or been, it is lying in the magical preservation of a book". With this quotation in mind the first of countless visits to local reference libraries took place. Fortunately, someone had the foresight to preserve on microfilm several different titles of local newspapers. This enabled the author to effectively turn back the clock to the halcyon summer of 1914. The reading of these bi-weekly publications made sombre reading, however this tedious and extremely time consuming task was occasionally enlivened by the occasional news report or grainy photographic image, relating to a former Leasowe, Saughall Massie or Moreton stalwart. As a result of press appeals for relevant information several local residents searched through their bundles of old photographs, preserved for posterity in old biscuit tins or battered dusty albums. To these kind people who loaned for copying, or donated treasured items, thank you for your much appreciated help, and for the added interest your family heirlooms have given this project. All loaned photographs reproduced in this work are acknowledged, items bearing no credit are from my archive. I also wish to thank the following people Geoff. Crump, Mrs. Barbara Jones, Dennis Reeves of the Liverpool Scottish Museum Trust, and Peter Threlfall who have helped the author with encouragement and more importantly information on matters civilian and military, each has equally contributed freely of their knowledge and time so it seems only fair to list their assistance in alphabetical order. Finally the resources and staff of Birkenhead and Wallasey Reference Libraries as without their archives and facilities this book would not exist.

This work is written from the heart and is an unashamed tribute to our local heroes.

3

Moreton and Districts Patriots 1914-1919

KNOWN DEATHS IN CHRONOLOGICAL ORDER

This listing highlights the severe casualty rates, the dates of which nearly all correspond with one of the set piece battles, which were staged in an often futile effort to break the stalemate of trench warfare. For example the summer to autumn deaths of 1916 all relate to the slaughter that was the infamous battle of the Somme, while the spring of 1918 deaths are a result of the German spring offensive. Most of these battles can be traced in the footsteps of the fallen Moreton Patriots, whose final resting places are dispersed throughout the globe, however most of the lives were sacrificed along the 650 mile trench system of the Western Front. During the quiet periods when neither side attacked, the average British infantry battalion lost an average of thirty men a month, mainly due to the unsanitary conditions of trench warfare. Men died total unnecessary deaths from illnesses like influenza, pneumonia, food poisoning or even frost bite, while the ever present snipers could also dispense death or wounds. The General staff who were often unaware of the conditions suffered by their men, accepted these wholly unnecessary deaths, simply regarding them as natural wastage.

The tragic effect on the inhabitants of the village is not hard to imagine, as each family braced themselves continually dreading notification of the loss of one of their menfolk. The deaths are representative of the casualties suffered by cities, towns and villages throughout the nation, the spiralling casualties gravely affected the nations morale. In the final year of the war government censorship concealed the extent of servicemen's deaths, as a result 1918 has proved the hardest for the author to research.

The following abbreviations are used to denote the nature of an individual's death. K.I.A. denotes killed in action, for example in a battle. D.O.W. denotes a combatant who died as a result of being mortally wounded. While DIED relates to a person who died accidentally, or as the result of illness, dysentery is a prime example.

WILLIAM MASSEY.	KIA.	24-8-14.
W. DENIS WILSON	KIA	16-6-15
CHARLES D WOODWARD	KIA	20-6-15
ERIC C. BARCLAY	KIA	25-9-15
EDWARD DAVIES	DOW	25-9-15

4

JOHN STANLEY	DOW	17-11-15
ROY BORROWMAN	DIED	7-12-15
CHARLES H. SMITH	KIA	19-3-16
JOSEPH V. ASHCROFT	KIA	21-4-16
THOMAS H. WARING	KIA	11-5-16
HERBERT G. SMITH	DOW	17-5-16
ALEXANDER M. WLSON	KIA	14-7-16
HERBERT BOSTOCK	DOW	22-8-16
ERNEST HARDCASTLE	DOW	16-9-16
PERCY SMITH	DOW	13-10-16
GEORGE PARKINSON	DIED	12-11-16
HERBERT H. HARRIS	DOW	28-3-17
CHARLES R. HARRIS	DIED	4-5-17
DANIEL STANLEY	KIA	7-6-17
ARTHUR G. BAIRD	DIED	1-8-17
JOSEPH SUTTON	KIA	10-4-18
OSWALD HARDCASTLE	KIA	11-4-18
JOSEPH EVANS	KIA	13-4-18
GEORGE R.E. LLOYDD	DOW	15-4-18
JOHN W. FRENCH	KIA	22-4-18
GEORGE E. ENNION	DOW	28-4-18
ANDREW BOWMAN	KIA	29-4-18
HENRY WILSON	DOW	31-7-18
ADRIAN P. LATHAM	KIA	21-9-18
FREDERICK S. CLARK	KIA	14-10-18
W.A. HERBERT MERCER	KIA	23-10-18
JAMES Y. HEATLEY	DIED	15-12-18
WILLIAM SMITH	DIED	29-1-19
NEWTON PRICE	DIED	8-10-19

Along the Western Front the rumble of the guns finally ceased on the 11-11-1918 but the war was not officially over. The Prime Minister announced in the House of Commons that 1-9-21 was the date when the war would be officially over. This was primarily due to the differences in Siberia and the relationship of Greece and Turkey. This timeline encompasses all the above deaths, it should be remembered that thousands of servicemen died throughout the austere 1920s. These brave men endured a prolonged living death, arising from their war wounds or gas poisoning.

The autobiographies of the following casualties include brief details relating to the day of their final battle or action. The concise battle details are purely to serve as a perspective in which to place the Moreton Patriot, while recording for posterity the scenario in which he gave his life. It has proven very difficult to condense the particular section of these huge complicated battles, which often failed due to their complexity. For clarity the battle detail often relates only to the battalion containing the Wirral man, this provides the reader with specific information concerning the local mans demise. For further reading there are numerous books available dedicated to a particular engagement, which was often conducted over several weeks or months.

During the Great War an infantry Division consisted of 585 Officers and 17,488 Non Commissioned Officers [N.C.Os.] and Other Ranks [O.Rs]. The Division was sub divided into 3 Brigades of 4 battalions each. In 1915 a 13th battalion of Pioneers was added. A County battalion consisted of 36 Officers and 1,000 men, but the actual fighting strength was normally only 800 men. The battalion consisted of 4 Companies of 240 men, divided into 4 platoons of 60 soldiers. A Platoon was then divided into four sections of 15 men. The strength of all the units decreased as the war progressed.

The ROLL of HONOUR

IS YOUR NAME on a ROLL of HONOUR ?

IF YOUR NAME goes down on your firm's Roll of Honour, it also goes on that mighty Scroll which records the names of all who have rallied round the Flag.

There is room for your name on the Roll of Honour.

Ask your employer to keep your position open for you. Tell him that you are going to the help of the Empire. Every patriotic employer is assisting his men to enlist, and he'll do the right thing by you.

Tell him NOW—

Your King and Country Want you——TO-DAY.

At any Post Office you can obtain the address of the nearest Recruiting Office.

GOD SAVE THE KING.

GREAT WAR DEATHS COMMEMORATED ON THE MORETON MEMORIALS

E.C. BARCLAY	MECHANISED MACHINE GUN SERVICE
A.G. BAIRD	ROYAL NAVAL RESERVE
R. BORROWMAN	KINGS OWN SCOTTISH BORDERERS
A. BOWMAN	3rd CHESHIRE REGIMENT
H. BOSTOCK	9th CHESHIRE REGIMENT
F.S. CLARK	10th KINGS LIVERPOOL REGIMENT
E. DAVIES	KINGS ROYAL RIFLES
G.E. ENNION	8th SOUTH LANCASHIRE REGIMENT
J. EVANS	2nd SOUTH LANCASHIRE REGIMENT
J.W. FRENCH	ROYAL WELSH FUSILIERS
E. HARDCASTLE	9th CHESHIRE REGIMENT
O.W. HARDCASTLE	13th CHESHIRE REGIMENT
A.P. LATHAM	10th KINGS LIVERPOOL REGIMENT
W. MASSEY	1st CHESHIRE REGIMENT
W.A.H. MERCER	1st. SOUTH WALES BORDERERS
W. SMITH	ROYAL AIR FORCE
H.G. SMITH	13th CHESHIRE REGIMENT
P. SMITH	11th CHESHIRE REGIMENT
D. STANLEY	11th CHESHIRE REGIMENT
J. STANLEY	11th CHESHIRE REGIMENT
J. SUTTON	11th CHESHIRE REGIMENT
T.H. WARING	KINGS OWN SCOTTISH BORDERERS
A.M. WILSON	2nd SOUTH AFRICAN REGIMENT
W.D. WLSON	10th KINGS LIVERPOOL REGIMENT
H. WILSON	4th CHESHIRE REGIMENT

Although the following names are not included on either of the village memorials they are included in this work as they are either interred or commemorated within Christ Church grave yard.

J. ASHCROFT	5th KINGS LIVERPOOL REGIMENT
A.D. BOUSFIELD	
C.R. HARRIS	4th CHESHIRE REGIMENT
H.H. HARRIS	12th KINGS LIVERPOOL REGIMENT
J.Y. HEATLEY	1st KINGS ROYAL RIFLES
G.R.E. LLOYDD	10th KINGS LIVERPOOL REGIMENT
C.H. SMITH	13th WELSH REGIMENT
C.D. WOODWARD	7th KINGS LIVERPOOL REGIMENT
G. PARKINSON	ROYAL WELSH FUSILIERS
N. PRICE	3rd LANCASHIRE FUSILIERS

THE HISTORY OF MORETON

Located in the North West of England, lies the Wirral Peninsula, whose boundaries are clearly defined by the geographical features, of the River Mersey, the opposite side of the peninsula is bordered by the tranquil River Dee. Both of these wide rivers flow into the Irish Sea. Consequently the Wirral is surrounded on three sides by water. The major town on the Wirral is Birkenhead which lies on the banks of the Mersey facing Liverpool. Due to modern boundary reforms Wirral is now classified as a part of Merseyside. The Wirral has traditionally been the western tip of the County of Cheshire. Its administration being directed from the walled Roman City of Chester. Some twenty miles away from Chester lies the coastal town of Moreton, which currently has a population of approximately 26,000 inhabitants. To the casual observer the town would appear to be fairly modern. This misconception arises from the piecemeal demolition of the area's old buildings, many of which were constructed from locally hewn sandstone. Their replacements were often constructed in Moreton brick from the local clay quarries. The oldest surviving building in Moreton can be found in Barnston Lane, the large farm house was constructed in 1719, some 450 years after the earliest mention of Moreton in 1272. The manor of Moreton is not recorded in the Domesday Book.

The above postcard dated 1908 shows Mary Anns Lane, todays Old Maryland's Lane.

During the reign of Emperor Claudius in AD.43 the Romans invaded Britain. Locally their main fortress was Chester which is said to have been connected to Meols by a Roman road. Troops were based in the area possibly as a look out for enemy shipping preparing to enter the River Dee. We know Romans were active in the isolated Moreton area as many Roman coins have been found locally.

Moreton, Saughall Massey and Claughton originally belonged to the ancient parish of Bidston, this formed part of the Barony of Dunham Massey. By 1328 the village name had been changed to Mortonemassey, the name now contained the manorial suffix Massey. In 1309 the manor was held by Hamo de Massey, the Massey family were also lords of Mortone in the thirteenth century. The spelling of Moreton constantly changed during the centuries. By the year 1549 Mooreton, meaning the town near a marsh now had its own chapel, like most religious buildings of the period it was built on a hill. Moreton hill later became known as Chapel hill, the site of the chapel is now part of a supermarket complex, the rise of the hill can be easily noticed when viewed from the roundabout looking towards Hoylake. The chapel was demolished circa 1690, a document of the time of King Edward VI lists fifteen churches and Moreton chapel in the Wirral Hundred.

In 1593 the first section of Mockbegger Hall or Leasowe Castle was built, for Ferrando the fifth Earl of Derby, who now held the Barony. The origins of the building is disputed, its purpose being either a lodge or a race viewing stand. For many years the Leasowes was the location of a highly popular five mile horse race. Another theory suggests the building was used as a stop over for the Earls of Derby when enroute to the Isle of Man. The Earls of Derby were virtually Kings of the Isle of Mann. The three legs of Mann are carved on the tower, above the date 1593. The name Mockbegger Hall occurs throughout the nation, where it relates to a rocky out crop or building which from a distance on a dark night gives the impression of an occupied and hospitable looking mansion. A beggar expecting a free meal would be disappointed to find the building unoccupied.

In 1723 Lord Derby and ten other affluent gentlemen agreed to subscribe the princely sum of twenty guineas each for a decade, to the races at Wallasey, which were held on the first Tuesday of May each year. This became one of the most important horse races in the country. The races were discontinued in 1732 when rising tidal waters flooded the course, resulting in the race being transferred to Newmarket, where the Wallasey Stakes were run for many years after.

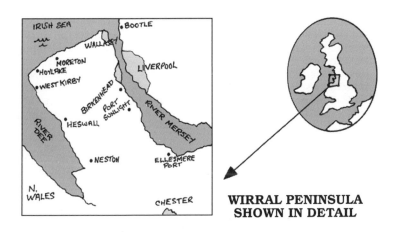

WIRRAL PENINSULA SHOWN IN DETAIL

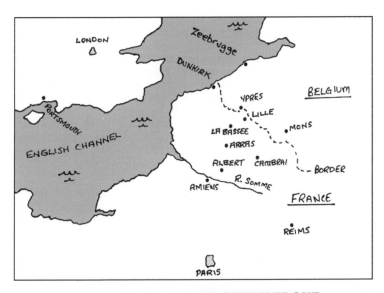

A SECTION OF THE WESTERN FRONT

In 1763 a pair of lighthouses were built at Leasowe, the foundations of the lighthouses are said to be built on cotton bales, which were recovered from a wreck. The cotton was considered to be the best substance to settle in the sand. Each lighthouse displayed a fixed light seaward, which was used as a navigational aid. One of the lighthouses was built on the beach nearly half a mile north of today's lighthouse. For a sea defence the seaward lighthouse had a barrier of high sandhills and mill grass, this proved woefully inadequate, the lighthouse was rendered useless by the advance of the sea and pulled down in 1769. The replacement lighthouse was built on Bidston Hill. The surviving Moreton lighthouse has recently been painstakingly restored.

Moreton cum Lingham, now meaning a farm near a long marsh had a population of 210 people in 1801. England' s first Saint Bernard dog arrived at Leasowe in 1815, and must have caused quite a reaction.

The western tip of Cheshire's coast line has long been associated with wreckers and smugglers. Some of the areas darkest deeds occurred in 1821, when the Dublin packet ship "Earl of Moira" foundered. She was laden with passengers, many of these were saved by the Hoylake lifeboat. Boats from the Wallasey area set off and plundered the vessel, any bodies washed up by the tide were stripped and plundered. In November of the same year "The Sally,' which was laden with cattle was driven ashore at Mockbegger. The exhausted ships crew stood guard until the evening, when they went ashore seeking warmth and sustenance. None of the locals were prepared to offer any hospitality, wearily the crew returned to their ship, only to find the wreckers had stolen everything. Many of the local houses now had stores of freshly butchered beef.

The village of Moreton was visited by a gentleman named Mortimer in 1845, he described Moreton graphically. "It is situated in a dreary flat, close to the shores of the sea, with roads excessively bad, and a bridge as dangerous to travellers as it is disgraceful to the county. It is in every point of view, an extremely poor village" Strangely he never returned for another visit. By this year the populace stood at 330, who resided in 88 dwelling houses, of these three were licensed namely the Coach and Horses, the Farmers Arms and the Plough and Druid Arms. The first three hostelry names are as familiar in Moreton today.

The quality of life in the village was gradually improving, one of the villages benefactors was William Inman of Upton Manor, he was an enormously wealthy man who made his fortune as a pioneer in steamship emigration. Circa 1863 land was donated by Messrs Webster of Overchurch upon which William Inman financed a church, rectory and school the total cost being £8,000. Unfortunately only Christ Church remains today, as a classical English church it remains as Moreton's finest building. The church is surrounded by a quaint cemetery which also contains the family vaults of its wealthy benefactors.

A decision was taken to build an embankment, as prevention against coastal flooding, this embankment protects over 3,000 acres of land. During the course of the embankment construction on 22nd January 1864 one of the workers discovered a male skeleton buried in a black peat bed. As the skeleton was discovered under the site of a sandhill, which was almost one hundred feet high and four hundred yards from the high tide mark, it was decided the body could not have been washed up. The bones were sent to London in March. A Professor Bisk lectured extensively on the skeleton. Peculiarities in the cranium indicated an original race or peculiar tribe.

The area of Moreton had always been somewhat isolated, this was remedied when the Great Meols to Birkenhead turnpike road was opened in 1841. Construction on the Wirral Railway began in 1840 this monumental task took twenty six years to complete. The railway originally connected the port of Hoylake with Birkenhead Docks. On 2nd July 1886 the station at Moreton was opened and the once isolated village was now linked to Birkenhead by an efficient train service. The economy of the village now faced an unexpected upturn with the arrival of seaside day trippers.

Due to a chronic housing shortage in the large towns, many of the visitors to Moreton decided to stay on permanently. As a result many of the local land owners allowed their fields to be used as camp sites, which gradually resembled shanty towns By 1907 over 1,000 tents were camped at Moreton, they must have provided miserable accommodation as the fields often flooded. The 1911 census returns revealed a population of 970, of which 474 were males and 496 females. The people were abandoning the slums of Merseyside for Moreton as the village offered low ground rent and no council rates. The tents were gradually replaced by wooden huts built on stilts, old tram cars or carriages were also utilised. The sites of these ramshackle dwellings were all located in the vicinity of the railway station, this enabled the campers to commute to Birkenhead or Liverpool for employment. Further inland the village was expanding, modern housing and shops now fanned out from the village centre. Amongst the builders was Tich Mason, a successful national hunt jockey. His prize monies, boosted by grand national wins, financed his property. Each building was named after one of his winning steeds, as can be seen on the small row of shops facing the roundabout.

In the summer of 1914 the annual Leasowe camping association sports day was held on Monday August 3rd which was a bank holiday. To the working classes the bank holidays were a luxury which provided a welcome break from the long twelve hour working day. As the sun streamed down basking the sports day participants in glorious sunshine, the conversations all revolved around the same subject, war! That night at 11pm Great Britain declared war on Germany and life would never again be the same for the inhabitants of Moreton, the nation and the entire world.

Above. Moreton campers solemnly pose for the camera. Circa 1915.

Photograph courtesy of Mr J. McGreal

13

THE ROAD TO ARMAGEDDON

The chain of events which preceded the first world war are diverse and complicated, the origins of the war began in the 19th century. The basic facts are Imperial Germany envied the colonies of France and Britain, which afforded both countries wealth and additional territories. Germany plotted and schemed in a variety of guises, trying to win over their far flung colonies. Throughout a very unsettled fifty year period most of the nations of Europe were involved in short lived wars, Britain had recently fought a war in South Africa, which concluded in 1902. The European countries which bordered Germany and her Austria- Hungary ally were becoming increasingly nervous of their hostile Germanic neighbours. A climate of fear of invasion prevailed, resulting in most of the European countries forming a series of pacts or alliances which would hopefully deter armed aggression. Undeterred the Kaiser continued his sabre rattling, while the continent started to slip towards the abyss of total war.

As an aftermath of the series of small territorial wars in Eastern Europe, many borders and territories were ceded which caused further continental discord. The small land locked country of Serbia was one of the countries which emerged victorious from the Balkan wars of 1912 and 13, the Hungarians now considered Serbia a threat. Despite all diplomatic efforts War now seemed inevitable, Germany bided her time, waiting for a suitable reason for armed aggression. Europe was now a time bomb ready to explode. In Sarajevo the capital of Bosnia, at 11 am on June 28th 1914 a young student named Gavrilo Princip shot dead the Archduke Franz Ferdinand, heir to Austria-Hungary, and his wife. As Princip and his fellow conspirators had travelled from Serbia, Austria-Hungary saw the murder as a plot orchestrated by the Serbian government.

Seeking reparations for the murders Austria-Hungary prompted by Germany made a series of demands on Serbia, who agreed to most of the demands, except for those concerning sovereignty. Britain proposed a conference to settle the dispute. However the proposal was declined by Austria-Hungary and as a result on the 28th July war was declared on Serbia. The following day Russia mobilised her troops ready to come to the aid of her Serbian ally. This precipitated a chain reaction over the following four days, as Germany declared war on Russia, followed by France, then invaded neutral Belgium. Britain issued Germany with an ultimatum to respect Belgium neutrality; while appearing to be Belgium's protector the underlying reason was an excuse to curb Germany's power, which was beginning to rival Britain's trade and maritime interests world-wide. Britain's ultimatum expired at 2300 hours on Tuesday August 4th. Immediately afterwards radio messages flashed throughout Britain's Empire "Commence hostilities against Germany". Europe was now at war in a conflict which would eventually claim 22,000,000 lives.

Surprisingly the declaration of war was enthusiastically received by the population of Great Britain, who considered Germany's vision of global expansion should be firmly curtailed by Britain. Edwardian Britain was a God-fearing nation, which rigidly adhered to a strict code of morality combined with a sense of fair play. Above all the invasion of neutral Belgium was considered to be contrary to these beliefs. The entire nation was unanimous in the opinion that a short and naturally victorious military conflict would reassert Britains' global dominance, by bringing Kaiser Wilhelms' armed forces firmly to heel. The majority of military experts considered the war would be over by Christmas. If they were wrong the nation would be in dire straits, as Britain's army was too small a force to engage in a prolonged European war.

The regular army was made up of highly trained professional soldiers, whose deficiency in numbers was offset by their tactical abilities. The majority of this elite force were skilled marksmen, whose main weapon was the trusty .303 calibre bolt action Lee Enfield. This small but formidable fighting force was ideally suited for suppressing colonial uprisings or home defence. However a prolonged war would literally bleed the army dry. Britain's military might was the huge armada of vessels which made up the Royal Navy, the world's most powerful naval fleet. The coastal waters surrounding the United Kingdom provided a natural defensive barrier; any invasion fleet breaching this watery barrier would theoretically be easily disposed of by the Royal Navy. Consequently it was considered unnecessary to maintain a vast army. Alas subsequent events were to prove the War Department drastically wrong.

Following the mobilisation of the armed forces the British Expeditionary Force [B.E.F.] safely crossed the English Channel, escorted by the ever vigilant Royal Navy. The Kaiser was unimpressed referring to the B.E.F. as a "Contemptible little army". This scathing insult was gleefully adopted by the old sweat soldiers of the force. The soldiers now referred to themselves as the Old Contemptibles, a title which still commands respect over eight decades later. The B.E.F. clashed with the advancing hoards of German forces near the small Belgian mining town of Mons. Undaunted by the superior military strength of the advancing troops, the British stood their ground. The enemy was scythed down with withering and accurate rifle fire. Such was the fire rate the Germans believed they were being decimated by machine gun fire. Having succeeded in halting the German advance, this gained the allies vital time to regroup. Now in danger of becoming isolated the B.E.F. made a tactical withdrawal. Their eventual destination was a location north of Paris, a distance of over one hundred miles. During the forced march of the famous retreat from Mons constant rear guard actions were continually fought.

The footsore, battle weary remnants of the B.E.F. eventually joined forces with the French army in a defensive position in the area of the River Marne. The Germans eventually withdrew. In an attempt to bypass the allied lines defending Paris, they headed north where they were again repulsed in the first of a series of battles at the Flemish town of Ypres. The soldiers of the opposing forces dug ditches for shelter from the murderous enfilade of rifle and artillery fire. These shallow ditches evolved into trench systems, which eventually ranged from the Belgian coast to the mountains of Switzerland. The Kaisers' troops had gained so much French and Belgium territory they could afford to withdraw. They selected countryside affording natural defensive positions amongst the ridges and villages of the undulating countryside. The invader converted every insignificant farmhouse or village into a network of citadels. This line of fortifications was named the Western Front by the Germans, who were also fighting Russia on the Eastern Front. The name is for ever associated with the massacre of a generation of gallant men. This front line remained relatively static for the majority of the conflict, although numerous set piece battles occasionally produced brief temporary advances.

On Tuesday August 4th the dawn broke over a nation engrossed in preparations for war, a well rehearsed military plan had now swung into action, within the home garrisons. The efficient deployment of the nation's army was vital, as not a day could afford to be lost if France was to be reinforced. Urgent measures were now required to bring the regiments up to strength. One of the immediate measures was the recall to the colours of men from the army reserve, these were military personnel who had left the services within the last five years. Also thousands of veterans of the South African Boer War now volunteered to rejoin their former arms of service.

In common with most communities Moreton had several residents who were classified within the two above categories. Tearful farewells were exchanged as sons or fathers departed to rejoin their former regiments or vessels. The families were extremely confident that the great adventure would be concluded by Christmas. As the first of the local men departed for their appointments with destiny, Moreton and District was reinforced by the military. The lighthouse at Moreton and Leasowe Castle were both utilised as a base for soldiers. The strategic heights of Bidston Hill were briefly occupied by the 6th Kings Liverpool's, prior to the arrival of the 3rd Cheshire Regiment. This reserve battalion also guarded the local docks, and other key installations and reminiscent of the Romans centuries earlier, had an outpost on Hilbre Island. These sites all formed part of the Mersey port defensive system.

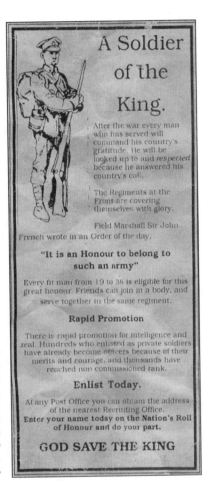

A Soldier of the King.

After the war every man who has served will command his country's gratitude. He will be looked up to and *respected* because he answered his country's call.

The Regiments at the Front are covering themselves with glory.

Field Marshall Sir John French wrote in an Order of the day,

"It is an Honour to belong to such an army"

Every fit man from 19 to 38 is eligible for this great honour. Friends can join in a body, and serve together in the same regiment.

Rapid Promotion

There is rapid promotion for intelligence and zeal. Hundreds who enlisted as private soldiers have already become officers because of their merits and courage, and thousands have reached non commissioned rank.

Enlist Today.

At any Post Office you can obtain the address of the nearest Recruiting Office.
Enter your name today on the Nation's Roll of Honour and do your part.

GOD SAVE THE KING

A minority of the Government considered the nation was facing a protracted conflict. A notable figure was the recently appointed Secretary of State for War, Lord Kitchener who envisioned a war of attrition, which would require one hundred thousand volunteers. Britain unlike most countries did not yet rely on conscription. Her army consisted solely of volunteers and the aim was for every County regiment to raise a new battalion. The prospective volunteers would be required to serve for the duration of the war; their new battalions were named "service" battalions. A vigorous recruiting drive duly commenced within the media parameters of the period, namely newspaper appeals and posters. The most famous recruiting poster was that of Lord Kitchener's stern face, above an accusing finger pointing directly at the reader. A caption below commanded "Your country needs you - enlist now". The recruiting campaign combined with the patriotic fervour of the male citizens provided the army with two million volunteers within six months. The citizen army of patriotic volunteers inundated an already overloaded military system, which failed to cope with the basic requirements of the volunteers. New army battalions were literally springing up overnight (A British infantry battalion consisted of almost a thousand men) and the Army Service Corps were originally incapable of feeding or clothing the new recruits. Initiative became the order of the day. Food was purchased from civilian caterers, and the men paraded in their civilian clothes. Most of the volunteers were originally billeted in school halls, tents or simply returned home to their families of an evening.

Uniquely in the industrial North West of England several prominent individuals rapidly appraised the problems facing the burgeoning Kitchener battalions. In late 1914 the Earl of Derby sought to raise a battalion of Liverpool volunteers for Kitchener's new army. His private recruitment campaign was directed at workers who shared the common bond of working together, in the same office or factory, or grew up together in the crowded City. These comrades were all assured they could serve together. The initial battalion became the nation's first "Pals" battalion. The concept proved so popular an additional three battalions were rapidly raised. The private army was initially financed by its founder, Lord Derby, prior to the "Pals" adoption by the War Office. The four City battalions were officially designated the 17,18,19 and 20th [Service] battalions of the Kings Liverpool Regiment.

The Pals concept was immediately emulated by many towns and cities. Gershom Stewart, the Wirral Member of Parliament, tried unsuccessfully to raise a Wallasey Pals battalion. His lack of success relates to the fact that most of the young men from Wallasey had already rushed to the colours. Undeterred the M.P. held several recruiting rallies, determined to raise a body of Wirral soldiers. At West Kirby a recruiting meeting resulted in only twenty-eight volunteers joining the colours. The disappointing figure was boosted the following morning when a further forty-two volunteers joined their departing friends on the crowded railway platform. A further forty-two recruits enlisted at a meeting held at Hoylake town hall, making a total of two hundred volunteers. On 1st September 1914 Lord Leverhulme appealed to his Port Sunlight workforce for volunteers, after which Gershom Stewart M.P. addressed the assembled workforce. The soap workers responded magnificently when over five hundred men immediately volunteered. The Wallasey and Port Sunlight volunteers combined to form the 13th [Service] battalion of the Cheshire Regiment. The Wirral battalion entrained from Port Sunlight to Chester, joining the Regiment at Chester Castle.

Not to be outdone by the recruiting success of his peers, Alfred Bigland, the Birkenhead M.P., raised a further two battalions for the Cheshire Regiment. This came about as a result of four Durham miners who travelled to Birkenhead. Enroute they had unsuccessfully tried at every opportunity to enlist. The stocky miners were deemed unfit for service, as their height was below the minimum height requirement. Mr. Bigland obtained permission from the War Office to raise a battalion of these men, dubbed the "Bantams". Within a few days over three thousand volunteers applied to join Biglands Birkenhead Bantams, enabling two battalions to be formed. These battalions were officially designated the 15th and 16th [Service] battalions of the Cheshire Regiment. Both battalions camped at Meols near Moreton, on an area where Stromberg's troops had camped prior to embarking ships enroute to the Battle of the Boyne two centuries earlier. The Bantams departed from Meols in June 1915 when they relocated to the Yorkshire Moors.

The over-riding concern of this vast army of volunteers was that the war would conclude before they could have a "Crack at the Kaiser". Amid the melee of patriotic men were numerous adolescents well below the services required minimum age of nineteen. A high percentage of recruiting sergeants were prepared to turn a blind eye to the recruitment of these baby faced youths. The under age volunteers sometimes enrolled under an alias so as to avoid detection by their anxious parents, who were in their rights to have their sons withdrawn from military service. The village of Moreton provided its fair share of under age warriors, at least one appears to have been withdrawn. The Nation's youngest known First World War battle field death was of a fourteen years of age Private soldier, while the oldest man to die on the Somme was 68 year old Lieutenant Harry Webber.

THREE MORETON WARRIORS

Few families were better known in Moreton and district than the Masseys, three members of which fought for King and Country. Sons of Mr and Mrs John Massey of Smithy Lane, Moreton, William the eldest was attached to the reserve section of the first Cheshires, and was reported missing soon after the Battle of Mons. Sydney recruited into the same regiment at the outbreak of war. Louis was an Able Bodied Seaman on H.M.S. Berwick, prior to serving on H. M. Submarine E53

W. M. Massey   Louis Massey   Sidney Massey

Any occasion involving the military regularly caused great excitement and the most mundane report often featured as a newspaper article. The August 12th edition of the Birkenhead news featured two reports regarding Moreton. The first article read thus. *"There was considerable excitement just before 11am on Sunday, when in a drizzling rain, a strong detachment of the Royal Field Artillery passed through the village from the direction of Bidston and took the road towards Upton. There were many villagers out at the time the majority of whom were making their way to different places of worship. When the clatter of horses hooves and the ring of cannon was heard on the highway outside the parish church, some of those who had already taken their seats inside, rushed out to the gates to see the passing soldiers. Such was the interest the service was considerably delayed, resulting in the late comers becoming the rule rather than the exception to this particular service."*

The clergy of all denominations fully endorsed the call to arms and on the first Sunday of the war from pulpits throughout the nation the clergy confirmed the conflict was a *just* war. The Rector of Moreton, the Reverend W.J. Spink, in the course of his sermon said that no matter what term might be applied to him for saying it, he firmly believed that God would be on the side of Britain in this horrible conflict. The people of these islands had always turned their faces and taken up arms against all tyranny and oppression on the part of foreign powers in the past, and in doing so they would not fail to be carrying out the will of God. The Rector was unaware that the German soldier also considered himself to be carrying out the will of God. The German infantry soldier wore a leather belt, the buckle of which bore the legend "*Gott mit uns*" or God is with us.

On 26th August the 2nd Corps of the British Expeditionary Force [BEF] under the command of General Sir Smith Dorrien while on the retreat from Mons, turned and made a stand against the German First Army near the village of Le Cateau. The heroic action cost the BEF dearly as approximately 8,000 casualties were sustained. The progress of the BEF had been reported in great detail in the press, the Jingoistic articles were now replaced with sombre reports of battles fought against overwhelming odds. The local papers gave brief details of the engagements, which concluded with a brief listing of local men who had made the supreme sacrifice. As break downs in communications were frequent the concerned next of kin anxiously scoured the newspapers searching for information relating to their loved one's battalion or naval vessel. The concluding roll of honour often gave the first intimation of the demise or fate of a loved one, although the families always lived in the hope, gaining consolation from the thought that their relation had survived and was now a prisoner of war. Within the village of Moreton concern was expressed over various reports that one of the Moreton residents, Private William Massey, had not been seen since the 1/Cheshires engagement at Le Cateau.

Undeterred by the rising casualties reports, the New Army continued to attract a multitude of volunteers. The Birkenhead News reported that by the beginning of October between twenty to thirty Moreton men had joined the colours, a week later a further ten men volunteered to join their comrades in Kitcheners New Army. The civilian population considered it to be their patriotic duty to provide home comforts for the men fighting for King and country, and legions of women beavered away knitting socks, scarves and gloves or preparing bandages. The Parish of

Moreton concentrated its efforts on the formation of an unusual Patriotic Fund, which was in effect a locally administered tax on the villagers who pledged to subscribe to the scheme.

Within days of the onset of war several of Moreton's older residents gathered one Wednesday evening with the object of raising a fund to assist the wives and dependants of those men called upon to join the regiments. A committee was formed of the following residents, W.H. Rudkin ~ Secretary, W. Briscoe ~ Chairman, E.J. Meadows and W.J. Rimmer ~ Joint Treasurers, Captain W. Smith ~ Assistant Secretary. Messrs G. Meadows, T. Kenney, W.M. White, A. Wilson and Mr Wilkinson completed the committee. The committee then appealed to the villagers to obtain a subscription card and then subscribe the sum of 2d [1p] to the fund each week. Such was the response the fund was able to not only provide financial assistance to the families whose major bread winner had joined up, it was also able to provide travel expenses for wives or mothers who wished to visit their wounded men folk, should they be a patient in a United Kingdom hospital. Any person who considered they were a deserving cause was invited to apply to the Honourable Treasurer Mr E.J Meadows, who in turn presented the application for approval by the fund's committee. An immensely strong community spirit was shared by the villagers, who magnificently supported the fund raising efforts of the fund. When a family pledged a weekly contribution to the fund, this was collected on the door step by the fund's Treasurers. The funds finances were regularly boosted by a series of fund raising bazaars and similar charitable events. One such event became the social event of October when a grand charity concert was held at the Moreton Assembly rooms. The building was filled to capacity resulting in many local residents being turned away. The fortunate residents inside the Assembly Rooms were entertained by popular vocalists who sang an extensive repertoire of popular patriotic songs of the day. The event proved a huge success both socially and financially, as the concert proceeds raised a further eighteen pounds towards the fund; this was a considerable amount of money in the autumn of 1914. For a financial comparison it should be considered that the Private soldier earned a lowly shilling (5p) a day, therefore it would have taken him almost a year to earn the sum raised.

Throughout the Autumn more and more men idled away their last few days before military life beckoned and they took their leave from the village. One such individual was Harold Briscoe a member of the Moreton Parish Council who had recently joined the colours and was waiting for orders to proceed to the

Headquarters. During a Parish Council meeting a telegram was handed in for Mr Briscoe instructing him to report to the Headquarters of the Denbighshire Hussars the following morning. The Hussars were mounted on horses, in military circles these were now a scarce commodity despite the fact they were still the main source of transport for the armed forces. The army had not fully embraced the developments in motorised transport, and still relied heavily on the more traditional source of horse power. Consequently the army now invoked special military wartime powers. This enabled the requisition of vehicles and more importantly, horses in private ownership. Over 375,000 of these conscripted equines were killed during the hostilities.

Photograph reproduced courtesy of Mrs P. Hoare, whose father is the Referee.

In the halcyon days prior to the war, five local lads participate in the noble art of boxing. Only three of the youths have been identified, from left to right they are~

Unknown ~ Eric Mutch ~ William Stanley ~ Unknown ~ Herbert Gardner Smith.

The photograph was taken on the site of the present Oakenholt Road Clinic. The site was a regular venue for boxing contests. The building containing the Assembly Rooms is prominent in the background.

Towards the end of 1914 an acute case of paranoia beset the country. This was brought about by the Government in the interests of national security. Part of the strategy involved the arrest and subsequent detention in secure accommodation, of people known to be of German ancestry. These unfortunate people were classed as aliens, and were considered to be part of a network of spies passing on troop and ship movements to the Kaiser. The extreme measures were considered justified following the capture of a German spy, who was later executed at the Tower of London. The junior Naval Officer, Carl Hans Lody was the first of eleven spies who were tried then executed by firing squad. The nation-wide alert was especially vigilant in the proximity of the sea ports. On Saturday 4th December the ladies of the Moreton Golf Club witnessed a stranger strolling around the area, jotting down notes. He then approached one of the ladies and requested a glass of milk. The lady refused to supply the milk, as the man had not been introduced by a member. The lady golfers decided the mysterious stranger was a German spy. A message was promptly sent to the soldiers garrisoned at the nearby Leasowe Castle. The troops rushed out of the Castle and made a thorough search of the area. When the search party discovered the stranger he was found to be still compiling notes in his battered note book. The man was promptly arrested but his fate is unknown. Rumours abounded that the stranger had wandered from an institution. This was given credence by the fact that a self respecting spy would not wish to be witnessed so openly compiling notes, in such a conspicuous manner. About this time a more serious event took place upon Bidston Hill, close to the Army camp, where a suspected spy was challenged by a night sentry. The intruder escaped to the confines of the surrounding wood. Despite an extensive search of the closely wooded hill, the man managed to evade the searchers. In the darkness one of the search party tripped over a fallen branch' and accidentally discharged his rifle. His comrades assumed they were under attack and opened fire. In the ensuing pandemonium a young Liverpool Territorial soldier was mortally wounded, Private Louis Morice succumbed to his wounds within a few minutes.

Other wounded soldiers were far more fortunate, the chilly month of November brought the return of the first of Moreton's war wounded. These men had received what they called a "Blighty wound", a wound which necessitated a return to dear old Blighty [Britain] for hospital treatment or a medical discharge. The soldiers were injured during the fierce fighting in defence of the Belgium town of Ypres. The press reported in depth the return of the wounded warriors. The earliest recorded newspaper report of a wounded Moreton man, was graphically reported in the 18-11-14 edition of the Birkenhead News.

MORETON SOLDIER WOUNDED AT YPRES.

Amongst those invalided home after the terrible fighting at Ypres is Mr. J. Lester, of Moreton. Lester who is a Corporal in the First Cheshires was attached to the National Reserve, and was called up immediately after the outbreak of the war. He was in the fighting line for some time before being wounded in the right hand, with a bullet, which pierced his overcoat cuff and firmly lodged in the thick muscle at the base of the thumb. It will be some time before he is able to use the hand. The bullet has not been extracted. He was wounded last Friday week and arrived home a few days later. He says "We have a big job to do over there" and thinks we shall need every available man if victory is to be assumed and that soon.

In early December the fate of another Moreton soldier was reported extensively.

AFRED JONES.

PRIVATE   1/ ROYAL WELCH FUSILIERS.

Alfred Jones was a veteran soldier who had fought in the South African Boer War. After leaving the army he gained employment on the Wirral Railways. Mr Jones worked as a porter at Park Station, Birkenhead where he was described as a popular employee. He was a resident of Moreton and resided with his wife Alice and family at 18 Stanford Road [now renamed Willaston Road].

As soon as war was declared, the forty year old veteran rejoined his former regiment which formed part of the B.E.F. and within weeks the regiment was involved in the turmoil abroad. On 19th October the battalion withdrew to trenches at Zonnebeke, Flanders. The following morning hostile artillery pulverised their new position, shell and rifle fire continuing until 10pm. The Fusiliers suffered over 100 casualties. The intense shelling recommenced the next morning. In parts of the line the adversaries were approximately 100 yards apart, and this short range combined with the accuracy of the Gunners, demolished the trenches. At 3-30 the beleaguered defenders received the order "To hold the line at all costs". Most of the trench system was now untenable due to the bombardment; by 6pm the line was severed in parts. Parties of isolated Fusiliers were captured. A secondary line was taken up 250 yards to the rear of the blown in trenches, and all available troops were arranged for its defence. As his company were retiring from the trenches to take up this new position Private Jones was wounded. He sustained a gun shot wound to the leg, below the knee resulting in him being unable to follow his comrades. He lay in the trench for two hours, before being found by his comrades who carried him to the relative safety of a railway embankment. He lay there along with other wounded from Wednesday to Saturday, when they were picked up by French ambulance men, and taken to the base hospital, before being invalided back to England.

The battalion's records were lost in action and the following figures are a modest approximation of casualties incurred for 21st-22nd October. Officers missing and P.O.W. 15, O/Rs killed 37, wounded 80, missing assumed dead 213. Almost a third of Britain's pre-war professional soldiers were now casualties, but Ypres had not fallen to the Hun

On the 15th November while enroute for England aboard the hospital ship SS. Oxfordshire, Private Jones wrote the following short note to his wife.

They embarked at Southampton on that day, as yet he did now know where he was going. There were 650 on board the ship, which had endured a very rough passage across the channel, "and my leg has pained me very much in consequence",

I do not expect I will be called upon to do any more soldiering, and I frankly hope not. I hope you and the kiddies are all right, tell them they will get their Daddy very soon.

The following day he wrote from the 2nd General Hospital at Manchester asking for his wife and family to visit him. Some time later he was transferred to a hospital at Todmorden, which is close to the Yorkshire town of Halifax.

Death on active service was the least consideration of the rising tide of volunteers, who were actively encouraged to join the crusade against German oppression. The men who were reluctant to join the forces, were cajoled by women who presented the shirkers with white feathers, a symbolic hang-over from the Victorian era when the feathers represented cowardice.

The chilly winds of December heralded Christmas and the depressing realisation that the impasse of arms would prove to be a prolonged campaign, centred on the charnel houses of France and Flanders. The maelstrom of violence embroiled more nations, as Japan and Montenegro aligned with the Allies, while Turkey joined the Central Powers. From the far flung Dominions of the British Empire the King's subjects responded magnificently to the call to arms. Ex patriots from India, Australia, Canada and countless other countries rallied to the Motherland in her hour of need.

On 16th December the German naval fleet evaded the Royal Navy and for 42 minutes bombarded the defended port of West Hartlepool. The action resulted in the death of 112 civilians and over 200 wounded. At the outset of war the military conjectured the war would be over by Christmas - instead the war was over here by Christmas. Modern warfare now cast a grim shadow over the civilian population of the defended ports, including the Mersey region.

6th Liverpools marching through Saughall Massie Village 19/9/1914
Courtesy of Ian Boumphrey

In the early stages of the war the military progress of the Moreton volunteers posed few research problems, as the village lads served together as a group, whose exploits were keenly reported by the local media. The young men of the village and its surrounding area usually made a Wednesday evening visit to the Argyle Theatre, which stood at Argyle Street, Birkenhead.

On the Wednesday preceding New Years Day the Lads went to the "Gyle" as usual. Amongst other things they heard a first rate recruiting speech by Major Murray who asked if there were any "starters" in the audience. The first to respond was Joe Sutton, who stood up and announced that not only was he willing to answer the call, but that he had a number of pals both with him there and at Moreton whom he would guarantee to persuade to follow his example. A rousing cheer went up from all sides of the theatre as this thoroughly Moretonian declaration was made. It was arranged that the gallant Major should meet the patriots concerned outside the theatre after the performance. The meeting took place and to the Major's surprise he was asked to go to Moreton at a pre-arranged time the following day. The Major was assured that at least a dozen young men of serviceable age would be ready and willing to welcome him. The Major duly visited the village where he selected fifteen men, the following day fourteen men passed the Doctor. The event was considered quite an achievement, not only for the spontaneity with which it was conceived and carried out, but also for the large proportion of volunteers from the village.

The above appears to be the only recorded recruiting visit to Moreton. Prior to this visit upwards of thirty young men resident in the village had previously volunteered. Some attended a meeting at the neighbouring village of Upton, while others took the initiative themselves attaching to various regiments. The majority of the intake of Moreton "Gyle" volunteers were allocated to the 11th [Service] battalion of the Cheshire regiment, which was raised at Chester Castle in mid August 1914.

The fledgling battalion of raw recruits travelled south to the newly founded army camp at Codford St Mary, which transpired to be an open field totally devoid of tents and provisions. The regimental history of the Chesire regiment records that three officers visited the nearby town of Salisbury, where they managed to purchase the battalion's immediate requirements, which included much needed rations and a tent for every twenty men. Within the overcrowded tents the men slept on the floor, which was just bearable until the winter rain water logged the camp.

All the above are Moreton men who joined the colours as a result of a recruiting meeting held at the Argyle theatre, Birkenhead. They are:

Top row: William Duncan, Herbert Eastdown, Ernest Wilcox, Percy Smith, William Meadows.
Middle row: Tom Hardcastle, Harold Potter, Arthur Stanley, Dan Stanley, Percy Linfield.
Front row: Joe Sutton, Jack Cooper.

The men were now sleeping in mud, and blankets were a scarce commodity. The volunteers were still attired in a wide variety of civilian attire which was now bedraggled. The daily routine of the battalion consisted of daily route marches, interspersed by trench digging, football and night marches. The purpose of these vigorous exercises was to develop the men's fitness and stamina. The tactical mobility of the infantry battalion was totally dependent on its marching ability, motorised transport was rarely used. The excessive hours combined with the inadequate camp facilities provided a fertile breeding ground for discontent, enthusiasm was at an all time low. A neighbouring battalion deserted, this incited the 11th Cheshires, and one night serious trouble was narrowly avoided by the unprecedented step of appointing a spokesman and issuing the men with extra beer. The situation was considered so serious, the next morning a telegram was hastily despatched to Lord Kitchener advising him of the dire situation.

In response to the telegram the battalion was promptly transferred by road to billets at Bournemouth, now training began in earnest, lectures were given by wounded officers, and old muskets were issued for drill purposes. Ammunition was almost non-existent.

The transition from civilian to soldier was constantly aggravated by the burgeoning armies lack of resources. Improvisation became the order of the day. At the top of almost every new battalions stores request, were rifles and uniforms, which were the most noticeable shortage. A national shortage of khaki material compounded the shortage of military uniform; there was however a surplus of blue serge. This was utilised to provide a military style uniform for the majority of the New Army soldiers. This stop gap measure of a uniform was detested by the new recruits as the uniform resembled a postman's or conductor's uniform, which was hardly the uniform to impress the young ladies. The men of the 11th Cheshire's received their blue serge uniform soon after arriving at Bournemouth, and wasted no time in locating one of the many photographers who plied their trade at the army camps.

The picture postcard was at its height of popularity in Edwardian England. The local photographic studios were quick to capitalise on the soldier's fondness for photographic portraits, and printed the photographs in a postcard format. Naturally these postcards were sent home to the soldiers' families and sweethearts and countless thousands of these postcards still survive. Eighty years later these postcards remain as a black and white graphic reminder of proud Great War soldiers resplendent in their best military uniforms. On receipt of their son's photograph patriotic families arranged for the portrait to be printed in the local papers roll of honour, accompanied by a short notice. The newspaper editors were quick to capitalise on the trend for military portrait photographs, the Wallasey News for example offered readers the chance to purchase copies of the roll of honour photographs at the following rates 12 copies at 2/6d[12p], 25 copies for 3/6d [18p] or 50 copies for 5/- [25p]. Three generations later the aforementioned postcards and photographs provide the majority of illustrations in this work.

While Britain and her allies continued to fend off the German army, the nucleus of the New Army continued military training, while a steady stream of fresh volunteers gradually expanded Kitchener's Army. By mid-January a further fifteen Moreton stalwarts responded to the call to arms, taking Moreton's total of recruits to over sixty. The amount of volunteers was considered a satsifactory response from a population of approximately one thousand residents, of which only a small percentage were eligible for military service. The latest boom in recruiting placed an additional burden on the Patriotic Fund as two of the latest recruits were married men, who departed knowing the officers of the Patriotic Fund would ensure their dependants were well provided for.

The Reverend William Spink also provided comforts for the wives left behind. The first of many social events was held on a wintry January evening when the spacious rooms of the picturesque vicarage were the setting for an evening of entertainment for the wives and mothers of the Moreton volunteers, the Reverend W Spink and Mrs Spink were the hosts. Amongst the ladies of the parish who attended were Mrs Barclay, Mrs Hylton-Moore, Miss Moore, Mrs Wilson Jones, Mrs Garland, Mrs George Parkinson, Mrs Parlett and Mrs Graham Smith. The evenings entertainment consisted of tea, followed by music, dancing and various games. After a light supper the evening concluded at 9.30 pm.

Towards the end of February the villagers attended the third Patriotic Relief concert, where the entertainment was again provided by popular singers. The attendance at the concerts were now starting to decline; as a result alternative methods were to be tried for fund raising. The rapidly approaching Moreton camping season was envisaged as a valuable source of revenue for the fund. The ladies of the parish readily agreed to provide a refreshment stall. This was sited on Leasowe common, where the ladies did a brisk trade selling home-made cakes, tea or hot water to the campers and day trippers. The first of May heralded the start of the annual Moreton camping season, the activities of this highly popular canvas camp were featured every week in the local newspaper. Early in the year it was proposed to draft troops to stay on Leasowe common where there would be "Plenty of fresh air for lucky Tommies drafted in Moreton". The lucky Tommies appear to have been the earlier mentioned Bantams who arrived at nearby Meols on the first of May, which just happened to coincide with the start of the camping season.

Throughout this year the maelstrom of human suffering and misery dispersed throughout the globe. The Union of South Africa conquested the German colony of South Africa. The military forces of Japan captured the Pacific Islands colonies of Germany. Italy entered the fray as an ally, while Bulgaria aligned with the Central Powers. Several countries remained neutral. The United States of America was the largest neutral to sit firmly on the fence until an infamous event shook Uncle Sam from his complacency.

On May 7th 1915 the homeward bound Lusitania was off the coast of Ireland. At precisely 2-28 the German submarine U20 fired one torpedo at the pride of the Cunard fleet resulting in a huge explosion. The vessel sank quickly claiming the lives of 1201 men, women and children; amongst the death toll were neutral Americans. The sinking became a milestone in history and set reluctant America on the long road to war. The crew of the Lusitania were mainly from Merseyside, the atrocity resulting in riots in Birkenhead. Stores with alleged German connection were looted or torched. Britain's inadequate ariel defences were exposed when a new weapon, the Zeppelin, brought death and destruction. Following the Zeppelin attack at Kings Lynn, Norfolk the nation now endured a nightly black out. The raid was witnessed by two Moreton Patriots, Sergeant John Fenlon and Harry Briscoe, who were in training with the Denbighshire Yeomanry. The Yeomanry were the horse mounted arm of the Territorial Force. In 1900 the Wrexham based Denbigh Hussars raised a Birkenhead squadron. This unit became known as 'D' Squadron, which was based at Cole Street, Birkenhead. Most of the original group of part time Cavalry troopers served in the Boer War. On the 5th August 1914 the Squadron was mobilised and were briefly stationed at Eccleston near Chester, later relocating to Bungay. The following May the Wirral raised 'D' Squadron was stationed at Beccles near Great Yarmouth.

SERGEANT JOHN FENLON

The year of 1915 remains synonymous with the death of innocence, a year when the old order faded away. Centuries of military protocol was discarded, as modern warfare imposed its iron will upon the shell pocked battlefields. It became an age when determination and raw courage no longer guaranteed military success. The deciding military factor in this new age of mechanised warfare was the machine gun. While a trained machine gunner could fire 600 shots a minute, at best a good rifleman could only manage 15 shots. The British General Staff were dogmatic in their outdated belief that cavalry reigned supreme in battle. It was still envisaged that a massed infantry attack of bayonet wielding soldiers would scatter enemy defences, enabling the cavalry to race through to victory. Unfortunately Kaiser Wilhelm knew differently. For many years his army had become highly proficient in the use of the Maxim machine gun. The pre-war Imperial army possessed Europe's largest amounts of this weapon. Unfortunately during the same period the British Army only purchased ten machine guns per annum. During the opening phase of the 2nd Battle of Ypres the Hun unleashed another weapon from their arsenal. As a gentle breeze drifted towards the Allied lines the German Engineers unleashed Poison Gas. Most of the terrified defenders of the Salient retained their postion, albeit at a high cost in manpower. In the following letter sent home from the Front, a Moreton soldier appears to lightly dismiss the mortal danger of a gas attack, he was certainly one of life's optimists.

A E WATLING

Corporal   1/Cheshires

Ernest Watling was a veteran of the South African war. During his military service he served as an armourer sergeant in an army cycle section. On his return to civilian life he was employed as the Sub Post Master of Moreton. He resided above the Post Office (now a pet shop) at Moreton Cross. Prior to the Great War he carried out part-time soldiering as a Lance Corporal with the 1st Volunteer Battalion of the Cheshire Regiment, which later became the 1/4 Cheshire Regiment which formed part of the Territorial Force.

Upon the outbreak of the Great War, he joined the National Reserve, and was allocated to the 3/Cheshires. He was stationed at Birkenhead for a couple of months prior to December 1914 after which he was moved to South Queensferry, West Lothian, Scotland.

Early in the summer of 1915, while serving with the 1/Cheshires in France he wrote a letter from the trenches, which is quoted below in the parlance of the times.

> *"It is quite a luxury to sit in a trench with the hot sun pouring on you. We are now in our 28th day in the trenches, and are beginning to look the worse for wear, and have lately had some trying and exciting times, have had a taste of "Kultur Gas" (which is not the penny in the slot type) on*

*several occasions. I often drop across to the 6/
Liverpools, they are a fine set of chaps, always
willing to do anything. We have at last turned the
corner, and are on the right road for Berlin, for we
don't appear to have the numbers opposite us that
we used to have. We have got them on our side
this time for a change, and the right stuff too. I
am hoping to see you in July."*

The above reference to gas probably refers to the German's first
gas attack on 23rd April during the second battle of Ypres.
Corporal Whatling survived the holocaust, returning safely to
his family. He later became the Moreton Post Master.

The year of '15 was a period when the British populace, military
and civilian alike expected a resounding victory over the Hun.
The majority of military strategists envisaged a total victory
emanating from the morass of muddy trenches constituting the
Western Front. The tantalising prospect of victory was further
reinforced by the capture of the German held village of Neuve
Chapelle. This was the year's first significant territory gain,
achieved at appalling loss of life to both sides. Beyond this now
forgotten French village stood Aubers Ridge, a key military
objective crucial for the next stage of the advance. The capture
of the ridge would pave the way for victory at La Bassee and
beyond, eventually leading to the fall of the German occupied
City of Lille. While the planned attack seemed so simple on
paper, in reality the task would prove an altogether different
proposition. Similarly within the infamous Ypres Salient the
defence of the Flemish town continued to devour a generation.
The soldiers of the Empire who had for months obstinately held
their ground, now made a partial withdrawal to a defensive line
closer to the town. An increasingly concerned War Cabinet
sought an alternative to the deadlock of the Western Front. The
solution was considered to be a direct assault on Germany's
ally Turkey. The First Lord of the Admiralty Mr Winston Churchill
championed a seaborne invasion to conquer the barren peninsula
of Gallipoli. A victory would also open up a Black Sea munitions
supply route to Russia, while the jewel in the crown would be
the capture of the ancient City of Constantinople (now Istanbul).
The consistent flaw in all of the new initiatives is best summed
up by a quotation of Frederick the Great "That we should all be
great Generals if we knew as much before a battle as we do after
it".

W. DENIS WILSON

PRIVATE   3483   10/KINGS LIVERPOOL REGIMENT

Denis Wilson was born in Bishapton, Renfrew. He had at least one brother, namely Alec, who features later. Denis resided in Liverpool, where he joined the ranks of the Territorial Army. The volunteer attested on 31/8/1914, serving as a Private with the regimental number 3483, posted to G Company serving at Edinburgh and Tunbridge Wells. The Scots background of Denis Wilson no doubt relates to his choice of regiment. The tenth battalion of the Liverpool regiment are perhaps better known as the kilt wearing "Liverpool Scottish". The Childwall based battalion has recently become a victim of infantry downsizing and faces disbandment. Their Officers Mess is decorated with several sketches, drawn by Denis Wilson who was a noted artist. The sketches were originally sent to his fiancee.

The new recruit was transferred to the second line, posted to the 2/10 battalion who were undergoing training at Weeton Camp, outside Blackpool. Due to an acute shortage of men, military training was by necessity brief. On Wednesday 20/1/1915 the first draft, including Private Wilson went overseas, where they joined the battalion serving in France and Flanders. Private Wilson was posted to Z Company of the 1/10 battalion, which was the senior territorial unit.

Five months after arriving overseas, the battalion were in Flanders (now Belgium). The battalion formed a part of the attack force which was in preparation for the First Battle of Bellewaarde. The object of this battle was to capture three enemy trenches, which were located between the Menin Road and the Ypres - Roulers Railway. The British went over the top at 4.15am on 16/6/1915 rapidly crossing no-mans land, capturing the German front line trench. Their new position was bombarded by the Royal Artillery, who thought the captured trench was still held by the Hun. Meanwhile, enemy machine guns within Railway Wood were halting the advance of V Company. The pinned down troops were joined by reinforcements from Z Company. To the tenacious Scots there remained only one course of action, both companies fixed bayonets and charged the machine gun postition. Despite the hail of bullets the position was taken, along with forty prisoners. The second trench was then captured, the new occupiers now endured an enemy bombardment. The seriously depleted force advanced again and captured the third trench, again suffering heavy losses. A small band of men attacked even deeper into the enemy held territory; they were never seen again. Attempts were made to consolidate the gained ground. Reinforcements were unable to reach the third trench, as the complete trench system was blocked by dead and wounded of both nationalities. The German artillery was now bombarding their lost trenches with over one hundred shells a minute. The remnants of the attacking troops were forced to withdraw to the old German front line, which they held until they were relieved. The action was considered a success, having gained its prime objective, the capture of the ridge, on which the first trench was sited.

Of the 23 Officers and 519 Other Ranks of the Liverpool Scottish who took part in the Battalions famous "Charge at Hooge" only 2 Officers and 140 Other Ranks emerged unscathed. The casualties consisted of 4 Officers and 75 other ranks killed.

A further 6 Officers and 103 other ranks were originally posted missing, later assumed dead. The wounded consisted of 11 Officers and 201 other ranks. During the famous charge of the Liverpool Scottish, 21 year old Private Wilson was killed in action.

Private Wilson would have been one of those posted as missing. Consequently he has no known grave. His name is commemorated on the Menin Gate memorial to those who fell in the Ypres Salient. Most of the old Bellewarde battlefield is now the site of a children's theme park.

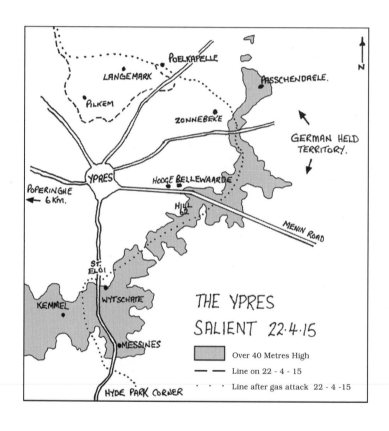

THE YPRES SALIENT 22·4·15

Over 40 Metres High
— — Line on 22 - 4 - 15
· · · Line after gas attack 22 - 4 -15

41

CHARLES DENNIS WOODWARD

LANCE CORPORAL   2535   1/7 KINGS LIVERPOOL

Charles Dennis Woodward was born in the district of St. Lukes Parish, Southport, Lancashire. The new born infant was named after his father, Charles Dennis. The confusion was further compounded when the son followed his father into the same occupation. They were both employed as Colpoerteurs, a rather grand title given to the labouring coal porters who carried the coal off the railway wagons.

Following the outbreak of war, Charles Woodward travelled into Liverpool and volunteered. In September 1914 he attested into the 1/7 Territorial battalion of the Kings Liverpool Regiment, which was unofficially known as the Southport and Bootle battalion. The battalion was based at 99 Park Street, Bootle. After rudimentary training the battalion was rushed overseas to reinforce the hard pressed BEF which was tenaciously holding the line in France and Flanders.

At Christ Church, Moreton wedding banns were posted, with their last reading on 21/2/15. The address of C D Woodward was stated as St. Alphage, Canterbury.

Prior to embarkation the thirty year old soldier was granted leave, taking the opportunity to marry Mary Sutton, a thirty year old Spinster. Mary was the daughter of John James Sutton, a local farmer, and the father of Joe Sutton, a soldier serving with the Cheshires. The wedding ceremony was held at Christ Church on 27/2/1915. The newly weds resided at 9 Airlie Close, Hoylake. The ink had hardly dried on the marriage certificate, when Private Woodward returned to his regiment.

The 1/7 Kings arrived in France on 8/3/15, the battalion served alongside the 1st and 1/5 battalions of the Kings Liverpool. The three battalions constituted a part of the 2nd Division of the 6th Infantry Brigade. The 1/7 spent the majority of March acclimatising to trench warfare, with occasional tours of the front line at Cuinchy. At the beginning of April they took responsibility for a small section of the line, where they sustained their first four wounded. The battalion was not called on for the unsuccessful attack on Fromelles, also known as the Battle of Aubers Ridge. However, the 1/7 were fully embroiled in the Battle of Festubert which raged from 15th to 25th May 1915. On the initial day of the offensive the 1/7 successfully captured the German positions. The following day an attempt to reinforce the recently gained trenches was launched. The advancing reinforcements were annihilated by concentrated machine gun fire. The battalion alone, sustained 9 Officers killed, 4 wounded and 220 other ranks killed, wounded or missing. The Kingsmen were relieved on 19th May, leaving behind 13 Officers and 301 other ranks dead.

Following an uneventful tour of the line, when the battalions were visited by Lord Derby, the Brigade was again relieved. Returning to the line on the 19th June, the Brigade took over the Cuincy Sector. The under strength battalions of the 1/5 and 1/7 alternated occupancy of a short front line section. The trenches were in close proximity to the enemy, often between 10 and 40 yards apart. The Germans were very active with bombs and rifle grenades in this sector, this factor appears to have a direct link with our Hoylake soldier. The following day proved an uneventful day for the battalion, with the exception of Lance Corporal Woodward who was killed in action on 20/6/15, approximately ten short weeks after his wedding. The only intimation of the cause of the soldier's death, probably the result of a bomb (early Mills Grenade) is contained in a letter to Mary. The war widow received the following letter of sympathy.

> *It is with deep regret that I am compelled to write to you in regard to the death of your young husband L/Cpl Woodward. It may be a light consolation to you to know that he passed away peacefully, and almost immediately after he was hit, suffering not the least pain. He was wounded in the back of the head, the left breast and the head wound causing death. He is buried in a corner of a nice little French cemetery, beside a little French village called Cuincy, about eleven kilometres from the town of Bethune. Your late*

43

husband was respected by everyone, with whom he came into contact, and I am sure I have lost a promising non-commissioned officer, and a good Christian soldier. You have my very deepest sympathy in this your hour of trial. God's will be done.

Sergeant A.S Brebner

The above letter was published in the Birkenhead News in the 3rd July edition.

Lance Corporal Woodward is now interred in Guards Cemetery, Windy Corner, Cuinchy, Pas de Calais. The cemetery is located at a cross roads, which was a popular target for German machine gunners. In the parlance of the times to "get the wind up" meant to feel fear and this possibly relates to the origin of the cemetery's name. The well maintained cemetery contains over 3,400 graves, marked by white Portland stone headstones. Amongst the neat rows of graves lies the remains of another local man 2/Lt Charles Henry Smith from Moreton. Although not a Moreton resident Charles D Woodward is commemorated on a Christ Church headstone along with his brother-in-law J. Sutton.

ERIC CALENDAR BARCLAY

LIEUTENANT   **MECHANISED MACHINE GUN SERVICE**

Eric Calendar Barclay was the younger son of Mr William C and Edith M Barclay, who resided at "The Homestead", Moreton. Eric was educated at Berkhampstead. On completion of his education, Eric Barclay was apprenticed to Messrs S M Bulley and Son cotton brokers and merchants of Liverpool. The young apprentice was said to be well liked with every prospect of a successful career.

Upon the outbreak of hostilities, Eric and his elder brother immediatley volunteered. Eric attested to the recently formed 12th (Service) battalion of the Cheshire Regiment. This New Army battalion was raised at Chester, and consisted mainly of Stockport volunteers. Private Barclay successfully applied for a commission, becoming a Second Lieutenant on 14th September 1914. Weeks later three vacanies existed for Officers at the Front, 2/Lieut Barclay again volunteered his services. On 21/11/1914, he was promoted to a Temporary Lieutenant, allocated to Number Three Battery of the Mechanised Motor Machine Gun Service. This new arm of the services was established during November of that year, under the auspices of the Royal Field Artillery.

The newly promoted Lieutenant arrived on the Western Front during the Spring of 1915. He was most likely involved in the defence of Ypres, and was mentioned in Despatches on 12-9-15. Almost a fortnight later during an advance Lieutenant Barclay was directing covering fire for our infantry. He was shot through the head, dying instantly on 25th September 1915. He was twenty years of age.

His mother received the following letter from the Front.

Sympathy is a poor word to express the feelings of the men who had the honour to be led by your son . A man's man, he was absolutely without fear, and no surer proof than the way he met his end. We were covering the advance of our men, and it was when looking over the front line parapet that an enemy sniper shot him through the head. I am pleased to say it was the sniper's last shot, for one of our men saw him perched in a tree, and had the satisfation of bringing him down. We buried him within forty yards of the enemy. Surely if fate had to be unkind, no finer end could any true soldier wish for, and though we miss him in person he will remain to us a memory.

Yours very sincerely
Sergeant Mackey and section.

As a result of his battlefield burial, Lt. Barclay has no known grave. The majority of burials on contested battle fields were often destroyed during a later artillery barrage.

His name is apparently recorded on the Royal Naval Reserve Panel of the Menin Gate Memorial, Ypres. The monument is a highly impressive and massive memorial to the 54,896 allied service men killed in the Ypres area, who have no known grave. Unfortunately due to the size and complexity of the monument the author was unable to locate the relevant panel bearing Lt. Barclay's name. The Menin Gate straddles the Menin Road, the memorial is sited upon the former site of a gap in the town's ancient walls. Through this portal the allied servicemen passed through on their way to the hell on earth that was the notorious Ypres Salient.

At Christ Church, Moreton during the evening service on Sunday 3rd October, the Rector (W. J. Spink) made special reference during the sermon to the late Lieutenant Barclay. The text of his sermon was as follows - *"Greater love hath no man than this, that a man should lay down his life for his friends" (John 15-13).* The Rector spoke very feelingly of the loss sustained by the death of this promising young Officer, who was well known and much esteemed in Moreton. The hymns 'Fight the Good Fight' , 'The Son of God goes Forth to War', 'How sweet the Name of Jesus Sounds', and 'Forever with the Lord', all very appropriate for the occasion were rendered by the choir.

Moreton was now a home to hundreds of wounded soldiers, who were hospitalised at the Auxiliary Hospital at Leasowe Castle. Towards the end of August a concert was held at the spacious City Caterers pavilion for the 450 wounded at Leasowe Castle. The war wounded were a constant reminder of the casualties of warfare and this combined with the ever rising body count depressed the Nation. As a result across the country the flood of volunteers began to reduce considerably. In an attempt to boost the dwindling volunteers the army raised its maximum age for recruits to forty, also reducing the minimum height by two inches (5 cm). Britain had always preferred a volunteer army, unlike the Continental armies where every male over a certain age was obliged to do military service. The dwindling manpower required drastic action, the solution lay with a certain Merseyside recruitment specialist. Lord Derby was appointed Director General of Recruiting in October of this year. He instigated the "Derby Scheme" which is perhaps better known as Conscription. Approximately 5,000,000 men between the ages of nineteen and forty-two were now ordered to register for military service. If the individual was medically fit he could enlist straight away in his preferred regiment, or he could wait until called up, and be placed with whatever regiment or corps required men. The married men were given the assurance they would be called up last. The Conscription commenced in the following January, but none of the conscripts arrived in France or Flanders until 1917-18.

T'was early last September
The country cried for men
And the men of Wirral answered
And said just tell us when.
We had not long to wait boys,
The order went right round -
Proceed at once to Chester,
Meet in the Castle Ground.
There were men from good old Wallasey,
And men from Sunlight too,
Who came with pride to offer
Their little bit to do.
It was hard to leave our loved ones,
Wives and sweethearts true,
Especially the kiddies,
Who will always think of you.
That night we left old Chester
To journey south again,
and every heart was happy,
T'was for Old England's name
We landed down at Perham
And then we understood,
T'was war, we'd have to rough it,
But still, it would do us good.
We were not long at Perham
Before we moved again,
Down to dirty Codford
Which drove us near insane.
Through slush and mud we laboured
And often got wet through,
Humping timber from wagons
For Jackson's building crew.
And when our daily task was done,
And we returned to camp,
We'd have to pick our way on rafts
To save our chests from damp.
With one false step, away you'd go
Out in the sea of slime,
Lost; marked, absent without leave,
This happened many a time.

Now we have had a tester hard,
It's often made us curse;
But we have managed to pull through
And now we're none the worse.
In fact, I'm sure it's done us good,
And soon we cross the sea
With every heart resolved to bring
Credit to Mersey and Dee.

Written by an unknown Private from 15 Section, No 1 Company, Wallasey
Pals. 13/Cheshires. Malplaquet Barracks, Aldershot. August 1915.

The following photograph is copied off a postcard, which the five
soldiers of the Stanley family and their cousin sent home. The
postcard predating September 1915 was posed for at a
photographic studio at Bournemouth. None of the men were
smokers. However one of them purchased a packet of five
cigarettes especially for the photograph.

Back row	Daniel Stanley	Herbert G Smith	
Centre row	William Stanley	John Stanley	Arthur Stanley
Front	Tom Stanley		

Photograph very kindly supplied by Mrs P Hoare

WILLIAM MASSEY
PRIVATE   7049   1/CHESHIRE REGIMENT

William Massey was a native of Moreton. The eldest son of Mr and Mrs John Massey, who had two other sons, Louis and Sydney. The family resided in Smithy Lane (now Netherton Road). When William married Martha Elizabeth they also resided in Smithy Lane. They later had a couple of children.

All the indications are that William Massey was a regular soldier. This is confirmed by his regular army number; also the first battalion of the Cheshires were regular soldiers. Private Massey was attached to the reserve section of this battalion. The regiment formed part of the original BEF which clashed with the advancing Germans in the opening stages of the conflict. This action resulted in Private Massey becoming the first Moreton man to engage with the enemy.

The 1st battalion arrived at Le Havre on 16th of August. The battalion was transported by rail to Le Cateau, were they waited for the rest of the BEF to form. The reservists spent their time in company marches, breaking in new boots and hardening their feet. The 1st battalion were visited by two of the top brass, Major General Charles Ferguson, the GOC and the Brigade Commander. The General Officer in Charge made a speech expecting every man to fight to the last man. Due to a mix up in the chain of command the Cheshires were unaware when the order was rescinded, and replaced with the order to retire.

As part of the 5th Division the 1st Cheshires were part of a flank guard, on a road leading north of the village of Audregnies, near the industrial town of Mons. At this location the greatly outnumbered professional soldiers made a brief, yet costly stand. The soldiers were such expert marksmen the accuracy and volume of their small arms fire led the Germans to believe that they were being scythed down by machine guns. The BEF successfully managed to delay the advancing invaders, gaining vital time for the redeployment of troops and the reinforcement of France.

Private Massey was posted as missing at Mons in October 1914. His family preferred to consider he was held as a German prisoner of war. Despite all the family's efforts, further information was unobtainable. The following year on 29th May, Mrs Massey was devastated by the arrival of War Widows pension forms from the War Office. The distress was prolonged until October 1915, when her husband was officially confirmed as killed in action. Private Massey had in fact been killed on 24th October the previous year. This was the day when the Cheshires first clashed with the advancing Hun at the French town of Mons.

Unfortunately Private Massey has no known grave, consequently he is commemorated on the La Ferte-Sous-Jouarre memorial. The memorial is located in the Seine et Maritime, 66 kilometres east of Paris. The impressive memorial records 3,888 names of missing men who fell in the 1914 Battles of Mons, Le Cateau, the Marne and the Aisne. Engraved on the monument are the names of 48 Cheshires with no known grave. Thirty eight of these valiant men were killed on the same day as Private Massey.

At Christ Church a headstone records the death of thirty year old William Massey and his brother-in-law Private Joe Evans. The headstone inscription states Private Massey was killed 23rd of August. This date is incorrect, and should read the 24th August. This has been confirmed in several archive sources. However, the most important considerations are that on the 23rd the battalion were digging defensive trenches, most importantly the first actions were fought on the 24th of the month.

On September 25th an Anglo-French attack was simultaneously launched along the Western Front. The French attacked in the vicinity of Vimy Ridge, while the British Army centred its attack at Loos. Subsidiary attacks were also to occur at Hooge, Poetre and Bois Grenier. The coal mining village of Loos, set within the Lens coalfield, where the flat terrain was littered with pits and slag heaps, was a defender's dream. The British Army's lack of sufficient artillery support, combined with the use of troops lacking in battle experience, was to be offset by the Army's first use of Poison Gas. Prior to the attack 150 tons of Chlorine Gas was released, most of which blew back into part of the British lines. However, two of the Scottish Divisions surged forward and although the Scots were decimated, the survivors managed to capture the village and even entered the second German line of defence. The morning's spectacular victory required immediate consolidation, by support troops, which failed to appear until late afternoon. The opportunity of a massive breakthrough was lost as the incredulous Germans hastily reinforced their positions. Strong German counter attacks eventually succeeded in winning back most of the lost ground; deadlock then set in. The village of Loos remained in British hands throughout the campaign, which was wound down in mid October. The Nations much needed first victory of the war claimed over 50,000 British casualties; the Germans lost 20,000 men.

EDWARD DAVIES   RIFLEMAN

R/6365   9 (SERVICE) KINGS ROYAL RIFLE CORPS

Edward Davies was born in Liscard, Cheshire. At the time of his enlistment he was residing in nearby Seacombe. He attested to the colours at Birkenhead, originally serving with 'C' Company of the 1/9 Territorial Battalion of the Kings Liverpool Regiment. Rifleman Davies later transferred to the 9 (Service) Kings Royal Rifle Corps, which landed at Boulogne on 20/5/15.

After serving at the front for some time Rifleman Davies was reported missing on September 25th 1915. This information caused great anxiety. A Mrs Jones of 18 Stanford Road (now Willaston) appealed in the 6th November edition of the Birkenhead News for any information regarding Rifleman Davies. Six weeks later the soldier's fate was revealed he had died of his wounds on the day he was posted missing.

The Kings Royal Rifle Corps Chronicle contains the most detailed report of the 9th Battalion's activities on the day of our subject's death. On 25th September the battalion moved out of the rest area to take part in an attack on Bellewarde Farm, north of Hooge, a subsidiary attack of the Battle of Loos. A graphic account of the day's ghastly events was reported by a Lieutenant R Holloway, 9/KRRC. The following information is extracted from his highly descriptive letter.

We were in action on September 25th supporting an attack. At 3.50am our bombardment started, and lasted for half an hour. The Germans immediately retaliated and gave us as bad as we were giving them. At 4.19 exactly a mine we had built under a German redoubt, fifty yards from our trenches was exploded. The bombardment made such a noise that the explosion could not be heard, but the ground shook very violently. The crater produced was about thirty feet deep, and ninety feet across from edge to edge. The mine was the signal for the 9/KRRC who were carrying out the charge to advance. This they did magnificently. They found the German front line abandoned, and advanced to the second line which was lightly held. They carried it and prepared it for defence, while some of their Bombers extended their left flank laterally, and advanced on the German third line. Heavy German counter attacks bombed the men of the 9th. They lost all but one of their Officers, and there was no organisation of defence. They had also lost 20 of their Bombers in five minutes in a very bad spot. Communications were bad, most of the trenches were blown in, and full of wounded men and this prevented the arrival of bombs and replacement Bombers. By 7.30 the 9/KRRC were forced to abandon the second line. This was due to the regiment on their right which had met with stubborn resistance, failed and left a gap. When my Company advanced the 9th were holding the German front line on our right, and we were to hold the crater and guard their left flank. At about 7.45am a messenger reported, shouting "Our shells are dropping short, right in the crater". Inside the crater there were more dead and wounded than living men. There was one machine gun in position. Almost as soon as I got in, one of our shells burst right in the middle of the crater, blowing several men to bits, a sickening sight. I gave the order to evacuate the crater, and to take up positions to the right and left of it. Before I left, two more shells burst in the same place. As each cloud of earth lifted, one saw men who had been sitting there alive just before toppled over, with shattered skulls and limbs, and blood pouring from them . We evacuated the crater and managed to get the machine gun away. At 10.00am we were relieved. Myself and a fellow Officer each carried a wounded man back to our trenches. I had bad luck with my wounded man, he was sniped on my back, covering me with blood. The rest of the day we spent under shell fire in support trenches, and at night we were relieved. We were shelled all the way back for about three miles. So far this was the worst fight we have taken part in. The sights we saw tried the stoutest nerves.

The objective of the battle had been achieved; this was to pin the Germans down to this particular part of the line, and to prevent their sending men and guns away from it. On the contrary, they had at least the 54th German Division against our Brigade, and our Divisional Headquarters and an estimated 48 batteries against our 13. The attacking force was outnumbered by a ratio of at least three entrenched defenders to one Allied attacking infantry man. The casualties in this sad affair were 5 Officers killed, a further three wounded. The other ranks lost 33 killed, 188 wounded and 29 missing presumed dead. Rifleman Edward Davies was recorded as one of the missing, who had died of his wounds during the September 25th attack of Bellewarde Farm.

The fortunes of war decided he shall have no known grave, his self-sacrifice is recorded on the Menin Gate at Ypres. The town was totally rebuilt after the war and is also known as Ieper.

During September the fully trained volunteers of Kitchener's New Army began to pour into France and Flanders. The 11/Cheshires, containing the small force of Moreton men, had also completed their long hours of training at camps in Winchester and Aldershot. The opening day of Loos was significant for the 11/Cheshires as this was the long awaited day when they finally crossed the Channel en route to the battlefields of France and

Flanders. The 11th Battalion served in the 75th Brigade of the 25th Division. The Battalion entered the front line during the early days of the Loos offensive where they held the line at Ploegsteert Wood, approximately 8 miles South of Ypres.

Meanwhile at home a growing band of politicians were expressing concern about the operation at Gallipoli. The military were urged to cut their losses and evacuate the deadly peninsula. The Generals advised that casualty figures resulting from such an evacuation would be catastrophic. As the Gallipoli troops plight became increasingly desperate, a seaborne evacuation with all its inherent risks was considered to be justified, because if the troops remained at Gallipoli they would surely die. The no-win situation would eventually bring about the only successfully planned operation of the entire campaign. The majority of the rescued soldiers were shipped to the Middle East, for the defence of the Suez Canal and Palestine.

JOHN STANLEY

BUGLER **22312 also 24514** **11 (SERVICE)**
CHESHIRES

Probably as a result of equipment shortages, Pte Stanley wears an absolete 1888 pattern belt buckle. Also notice, the rifle does not have a sling fitted. The back pack and ammunition pouches are missing as well.

54

The Stanley family were a long established Moreton family. Elizabeth and James had four sons, the eldest was John, who was popularly known as Chass. Prior to military service John was in the employment of a Moreton market gardener. In the early days of the war he attested to the colours at Moreton. He joined the original batch of Moreton chums serving with the recently raised 11th (Service) battalion of the Cheshire Regiment.

The battalion arrived in France and Flanders on September 26th 1915. The Regimental history of the Cheshire Regiment pays little attention to the arrival and initial activities of this war raised battalion of Kitchener's volunteers. Approximately seven weeks after leaving "Blighty" the 11/Cheshires were in front line trenches at Ploegsteert, Belgium. On the 16th November 1915 Bugler Stanley was on patrol duty, when he was shot in the back by a sniper. The mortally wounded soldier appears to have been evacuated to the hospital centre, located at the town of Bailleul. The French town is near the Belgium border, 14.5 km south of Ieper. Private Stanley's life was gradually ebbing away; the twenty seven year old died of his wounds the following day. He became the ninth member of the battalion to die overseas, a further two had died while training in Britain.

Private Stanley is interred within Bailleul Cemetery Extension, his grave reference is IC17. Throughout France, the communal cemeteries are the final resting place of citizens of the local community or commune. With the onset of war the consecrated ground was naturally used for interring deceased service personnel. The battle field carnage produced so many victims the cemeteries were extended, by the addition of an extra plot which is often in close proximity to the orginal grave yard. The Bailleul Communal Cemetery contains the final resting place of over 4,000 soldiers. This silent army was unable to rest in peace; the town was bombed and shelled in July 1917, and worse was to come. Following the Battle of Bailleul 13th - 15th April 1918 the town fell to the Germans for over four months.

The death in military service of Private Stanley is recorded on the family headstone at Moreton.

The splendid photograph of Private Stanley was very kindly donated by Mrs P Hoare, nee Stanley. Donations or copies of treasured family snapshots such as these are a researcher's delight.

MORETON NATIVE PATRIOTS

As already announced in Wednesday's "News", the latest native of Moreton to fall in action in France is private John Stanley, popularly known as "Chass", a son of Mr. James Stanley, of Moreton terrace. The above group was taken in Moreton whilst all the boys, who joined together, were on their final leave. The only one not presently out in France is private G. Davies, who is still somewhere in the neighbourhood, but nevertheless on active service.

Back row: Private D Stanley, Private G. Davies, Private P. Linfield
Front row: Bugler J. ("Chass") Stanley (killed), A. Stanley, Fred Thomas, F. Stanley.

Several of the Moreton men served with the 1/4 Cheshire Territorials who were based at Grange Road West, Birkenhead; their old drill hall is now a sports hall. The Territorial Force was purely a home defence force and as such the men were not obliged to serve overseas. However the vast majority of these part time soldiers volunteered for service overseas. Much to their disgust the part time soldiers were subjected to almost a year's training, and on completion in mid June 1915 the 4th Cheshires prepared for service overseas. Their destination was withheld from them but as tropical kit was issued the men considered their destination would be India. Along with their peers, the 7th Cheshires, they joined the 53rd Division which was due to board troop ships, their ulimate destination was withheld from the Officers and their men. Amongst the 1/4 Cheshires was Private John Percival Biddle, a Moreton son of the soil. Contrary to army regulations Private Biddle recorded brief notations of his war time exploits in a diary, a transcription of which has been kindly provided by his son Frank. The diary records that after a few day's embarkation leave the Moreton volunteer and his compatriots boarded a troop ship on July 16th, which sailed almost immediately. After replenishing stops at Gibraltar and Malta, His Majesty's Troop Ship Eurepides arrived at Alexandria on July 27th. A much anticipated furlong ashore was denied, instead to maintain fitness and as a means of preventing careless talk in the local bazaars the following couple of days were spent on route marches. The troopship's next port of call on the great mystery tour was Port Said, where the men had an opportunity to go for a swim, before sailing on the evening of August 4th for Lemnos Island. On arrival on August 7th their vessel ran ashore, the battalion was taken off at midnight by HMS Carrron. The next day they put into Imbros, sailed again and landed under cover of darkness on an undisclosed beach. A chance find of a discarded bundle of maps revealed the battalion was on the shore of "C" beach, Suvla Bay, Gallipoli.

The stage was set for their supporting role in one of the most disorganised campaigns this century, an invasion devoid of adequate senior leadership, where swift and assertive action would have overpowered the Turks. The next day despite their commanding Officer's objectives the Cheshires were hastily pitched into the day old attack on a formidable hill barrier named "Tekke Tepe". As they advanced across a dry salt lake under a hail of shrapnel and through a stream of casualties a Birkenhead Territorial complained "of being given better orders for a bun fight in Birkenhead Park". The Cheshires joined the lost battalions totally disorientated in a large scrub covered plain raked by hostile small arms fire. The following day under a merciless sun the attack continued and those who were killed or wounded were left to perish in the scrub which was now burning fiercely. These ill prepared attacks waged by brave but inexperienced infantrymen cost the 4th Battalion 9 Officers killed, 7 wounded and 20 men killed, 117 wounded and 289 missing assumed dead.

Approximately six weeks after arriving on the peninsular the recently appointed L/Cpl Biddle succumbed to an undisclosed ailment, the severity of which necessitated evacuation aboard a hospital ship to Malta, where the diarist was hospitalised for several weeks. He was discharged from hospital in early December and was spared a return to the Gallipoli beaches, when he was ordered to board a troopship destined for Egypt.

ROY BORROWMAN

PRIVATE   20197   1/KINGS OWN SCOTTISH BORDERERS

Thomas Rodick (Roy) was the son of Thomas and Emma Borrowman. For many years Emma was the licensee of the Coach and Horses Hotel, Moreton. The family resided at Braywood Villa's, Chapel Lane, Moreton. The Victorian block of three terrace houses has survived, although their grand title has fell into misuse. The Borrowman family resided in the corner house which is now 4 Barnston Lane.

Although a son of the soil, young Roy took an apprenticeship at the famous Birkenhead shipbuilders of Messrs Cammell Laird. Roy was employed as an apprentice Joiner, who was apprenticed to a Mr George Clark. The erstwhile artisan was desribed as a promising youth. As the Summer approached the young lad decided to exchange his bench for a trench.

In June 1915, Roy and two boyhood companions, Bob Hale and Tom Waring, travelled to Birkenshaw, Yorkshire. They then took the King's shilling and enlisted into the Kings Own Scottish

Borderers (KOSB). The first battalion of this border raised regiment, consisted of pre-war professional soldiers. The battalion had been embroiled in the Gallipoli debacle since the amphibious landings on 25/4/15. The Gallipoli campaign was originally perceived as a bold initiative to quash the Turks, who were allied to Germany. Capture of the Gallipoli peninsula would open a munitions sea route via the Dardenelle Straits to the Black Sea ports of Russia. However, the Army General Staff secretly dismissed the campaign as a side-show, which threatened their supply of munitions and men destined for the Western Front. The Gallipoli troops were short of most material items, but the most significant item absent, was a decisive and intelligent plan of action. The troops did have something in abundance - raw courage and determination to win at any odds.

The narrow Gallipoli beaches were virtually a holding area for a vast allied army. The ill equipped force was sandwiched between the Aegean Sea and lofty craggy cliffs. Beneath the blazing sun, the gullies and cliff tops were the scenes of pitched hand to hand combat. The casualties of these battles were abandoned where they fell, the deaths of the wounded men were frequently attributed to death from thirst. The wounded could not be recovered as sniping was a popular past time with both sides, any movement on open ground meant death. The unburied corpses provided a fertile breeding ground for swarms of flies, which then spread disease. In July, the allies were infected with dysenteric-diarrhoea, which spread like wildfire, mainly due to inadequate medical treatment.

Private Borrowman arrived on the disease ridden peninsula in October 1915. Winter clothing also arrived for the troops; however the clothing was returned to base. The first three weeks of November the peninsula was battered by gales. On November 26th a violent thunder storm heralded the start of 24 hours of torrential rain, which turned the trenches into watercourses. During this week 10,000 men were recorded as sick, Private Borrowman was probably one of these men. The freezing cold weather then arrived, soldiers froze to death, while over a thousand suffered frost bite.

A few weeks after arriving on the shores of Gallipoli, Private Borrowman contracted dysentery. He was evacuated by sea to the base camp an incredible 650 miles away at Alexandria. The eighteen year old youth died on 7th December 1915. He is interred at grave reference B36 within Alexandria (Chatby) Military and War Memorial Cemetery, Egypt. Chatby is a district on the eastern side of the city of Alexandria, between the main dual carriageway to Aboukir, known as Al Horaya, and the sea. The cemetery is open Saturday to Thursday 0700 to 14-30.

Three days after the death of Private Borrowman the evacuation of Gallipoli commenced. Each night under cover of darkness naval vessels sneaked inshore to recover troops and supplies from the beach heads. The remaining defenders successfully deceived the Turks into believing business was as usual. The last night of the evacuation was January 7th when the remaining soldiers were spirited away. The disastrous campaign had involved 410,000 British and Anzac troops, and 70,000 French troops. The British Empire troops sustained 205,000 casualties, of these 43,000 were killed or died of wounds or disease, 90,000 troops were evacuated due to illness. The French suffered 47,000 casualties, including 5,000 killed. The Turkish Army casualties are estimated at 250,000. The campaign achieved no tangible gain.

Anzac Cove, Gallipoli
A post-war snapshot of a typical beach head - notice the concrete blockhouse on the lower right shoreline.

Private Roy Borrowman was the last Moreton youth to fall in this year. The long awaited arrival of "Kitcheners Mob" boosted the failing esperit de corps of the ever dwindling Western front defenders. Their arrival came a little too late in the year to have any real strategic effect. The battles of '15 were constantly hampered by a famine of artillery shells. The nation's industry strove for an even higher level of productivity, despite a shortage of skilled manpower. A significant amount of key workers had abandoned their mundane engineering jobs, opting instead for military life. Initially their positions were filled by emancipated females. At nearby Hoylake in response to the shell shortages the Liverpool area's first non-profit making factory was established to produce precision engineered shell casings. The factory, which was situated opposite the railway station, produced a variety of shells, the total war production exceeded 121,000 shell cases. The areas industrial giants were naturally all involved in war production creating a boom time for ship repair and ship building. Large companies often diversified - the Lever Brothers soap factory at Port Sunlight also produced glycerine, shells and developed a military gas known at the front as P.S. The abundance of work offered good pay and entire families were now able to gain employment producing a previously undreamed of high income, much to the annoyance of the soldiers abroad.

Farmers Arms, Moreton. Notice the soldiers.
Courtesy of Mr. L. Clow.

Even the most optimistic person now realised the entire World was totally immersed in a bloody war of attrition, to be fought virtually to the last man. The public clamoured for news, the local press responded by covering in depth the military exploits of the sons of Wirral. Less welcome reading was the ever increasing obituaries declaring the sacrifice of one of the regions fallen. As a result the papers had insufficient space to report the more mundane day to day events occurring locally. One of the exceptions was Captain Smith whose marriage in late January was thus covered by the Birkenhead News.

The confirmed bachelors of Moreton will be surprised to hear Captain Smith has been married in St. Faiths Church, Waterloo. The bride Miss M H Pimbley of Crosby House Farm, Great Crosby, is the daughter of the late Thomas Pimbley. Moreton's hope is that Mrs Smith may occupy herself so largely with local affairs particularly regarding soldiers as her Husband has.

This benevolent gentleman's name appears sporadically throughout this project. He is believed to have been a retired Naval Officer who resided in Orchard Road.

The life sapping conflicts of the previous year have long been eclipsed by the carnage in 1916, which still remains as one of the blackest years in British military history. An insignificant river which meandered through the French countryside became synonymous with futile attacks and the flagrant disregard for brave men's lives. Eight decades later the infamous Battle of the Somme is perhaps the most renowed event of the war. Its notoriety is attributed to the appalling casualties. All too many of Great Britain's families sustained the loss or wounding of a loved one on the Somme. As a result the titanic struggle still remains as the best recorded campaign of the war. The year also witnessed other prolonged campaigns which have received little recognition or accolades for the military forces fighting in the equally important "Side shows" of the German Cameroon's, East Africa, Macedonia and a myriad of other exotic sounding locations. A few of the Moreton Patriots were now involved in diverse combat zones, for example Sgt John P Biddle was serving in Palestine, Horse Driver William Stanley of the Royal Horse Artillery served in Salonika and Private James Tarrant was a Motor Transport Driver in Mesopotamia. The majority of land based personnel were confined to the fringes of 650 miles of No Mans Land along the Western Front.

Along the Front the entrenched opposing forces continually attemped to wrest away a few square miles of shell blasted territory from the foe. Each side continually probed the other's defences, searching for a lightly defended sector which might prove susceptible to a massed breakthrough. This tactic confined Divisions of men to the tedium of front line duties, standing to at dawn and dusk, in readiness for an attack. Artillery continually pounded the front line defences aided and abetted by spotter aircraft, which occasionally dropped steel spikes or grenades on the enemy below. As can be appreciated even the quietest period in the line was fraught with danger. The periods in the line were regularly interspersed by relief periods out of line and hopefully beyond artillery range. The sanity saving reliefs provided an opportunity for de-lousing, bathing, rest and hopefully a visit to a local Cafe for a couple of beers or vins blancs. Frequently the resting troops were pressed into service, carrying supplies through the network of trenches.

Jan ~ 10 ~1916

Pte H Wilson. 3803
1/4 Batt Cheshire Regt
No 4 Platoon. 53 Division
159 Brigade. British
Force Egypt

Dear Sister

Just a few lines to you to say that I got your letter dated 24 June 1916. Sorry to hear abour Harry and Joe, hoping Harry will never see the firing line.

I have seen a bit of it and dont want to see no more I am alright now only I ham getting plenty of work have not much time to myself. I g cud tell you suming about Roy Borrowman but cannot he was very near to me when he whent away I surpose ——— kept well. I hope so and Father. I got a letter from home same as I got yours, it was miggie letter dated 24 of June ——— I got yours the same day. There where the ———leg to letter I have has not yet one from home and one from ——— tell Mary Robert I have not had any from her yet but I have written to her. Well I think this is all I can say at present.

From your loving brother Harry.

With love to all at home.

Transcript of a letter written shortly after the evacuation of the Gallipoli peninsula. The writer, a resident of Moreton, did not survive the Great War. The correspondent refers to fellow Gallipoli veteran Roy Borrowman of the KOSB who died on 7/12/1915. Due to censorship he was unable to reveal this fact. Courtesy of Mrs. V. Wilson

CHARLES HENRY SMITH

2 LIEUTENANT 13 (SERVICE) WELSH REGIMENT

Charles Henry Smith was born in Liverpool on 24th March 1890. His parents were Frederick Smith, a Post Office employee, and Ann Smith the daughter of William Young. The family later resided at 36 Seymour Street, Tranmere, Birkenhead. Charles was educated in Birkenhead at the Woodlands and also Lynams Academy. On completion of his education he was employed on the office staff of the famous White Star Shipping Line. He received rapid promotions swiftly becoming the Private Secretary to the Manager of the White Star Line.

In 1907 Charles H Smith joined the local Territorial unit the 1/4 Cheshires. At the commencement of hostilities the battalion was mobilised. In June 1915 he was promoted to Second Lieutenant attached to the Welsh Regiment. From the 10/12/15 he served in France and Flanders, serving with the 13th (2nd Rhondda) battalion of the Welsh Regiment. The young Officer was killed at Givenchy on 19/3/16, dying five days short of his 26th birthday. This area was continually swept by artillery as each side gave reciprocal bombardments. Although the death of this Officer was listed as a 13th Welsh casualty, on the date of his death the battalion was in Reserve Billets at Gorre and out of the trenches. He was most likley killed whilst attached as Brigade Bombing Officer to another battalion of the Brigade. A fellow Officer forwarded the following epitaph to the deceased Officer's grieving parents.

Your son was a worthy man and a gallant officer. We had been associated ever since the Welsh Division became a distinct force on the Western Front. We billeted together and during all that time he impressed me with his energy and activity. Let me say at once that to him the White Star Line was the idol of his old life, his connections with it he always spoke of as the glory of his work. Yet he kept a place for soldiering, he was proud to have been one of the first of the Liverpool Territorials, and though his commission attached him to the Welsh Regiment, he had always an affection for his old battalion, the Cheshires. Recently when the Bantams joined us for instruction, Lieut. Smith was untiring in his devotion. As you know he was made Brigade Bombing Officer, and in that position he brought bombing to a fearsome degree of perfection. His superior Officers had

65

a very high opinion of him, and it is no secret that he had daily to attend the Brigade conference, where his opinion was highly valued. He was killed unfortunately, on the 19th instant, by the explosion of one of our own shells, yet it was a daring audacious deed to be there at all, yet he would not ask his men to remain where he would not dare stay. Several were killed with him, because they must hold that little crater and keep it from the enemy. The sap is still ours, but some of those who held it are dead. We buried him on Monday in the presence of many friends, with the rumble of guns for a requiem. Anon.

2/Lieutenant Smith is interred in Guards Cemetery, Windy Corner, Cuinchy, France. The village is in the proximity of Givinchy, which lies approximately midway betwen Bethune and La Basse. This sector was captured from the Germans in late 1915. Germanic policy was to continually attack and regain any lost territory, a tactic which cost the Central Powers dearly.

The parents of the deceased Officer later resided at "St Malo", Glebe Road, and this address is thought to be 10 Glebelands Road, Moreton. Their last known address was 24 Westbrook Road, Moreton. Christ Church cemetery contains the family grave, the weathered headstone of which commemorates the death of the young volunteer.

JOSEPH WILLIAM ASHCROFT

PRIVATE   1883   1/5 KINGS LIVERPOOL REGIMENT

Joseph W Ashcroft was born in West Derby, Liverpool, the eldest son of Joseph and Mary. Prior to war service he lived with his parents at 52 Adelaide Street, Kensington, Liverpool.

On 4/8/1914 the 1/5 Kings territorial battalion was raised at 65 St Anne Street, Liverpool. Joseph W Ashcroft was one of the eager volunteers who served with this battalion. Following military training near Canterbury the battalion entrained for Southampton, where they boarded the transports Duchess of Argyle and Queen Empress. The vessels arrived at Havre (now Le Havre) and the troops disembarked on 22/2/1915. At Bethune the rookie soldiers were coached in the rudiments of trench warfare, by the old sweat professionals of the 1/Kings Liverpools. On the night of 14/2/1916 the 1/5 battalion, now a part of the 165th Brigade, took over the Ficheux sector, which lies approximately 4.5 miles (7.5 K) south of Arras. The retiring French Territorials had left their trenches in a dilapidated condition. The 1/5 Kingsmen spent the duration of February and March digging, deepening and revetting the trench system. Continuous heavy rain combined with a severe shortage of trench boards often rendered this physical and demoralising work useless. The month of April also proved to be an uneventful period for this particular battalion. It was during this quiet period that Private Ashcroft was killed in action, the cause of his untimely demise is unknown. The 18 year old soldier was probably the victim of a sniper's bullet or a random artillery shell.

Within the tidy cemetery at Christ Church, Moreton lies the grave of Private Ashcroft's parents, whose last known address was 37 Sandbrook Lane, Moreton. Their headstone also commemorates the self-sacrifice of their son who was "Killed in action at the Battle of Arras on 21/3/1916, aged 19". The month of March has proven to be incorrect, as the young man was killed exactly one month later, his age is stated as 18. Several independent archive sources confirm the date of death as 21/4/1916. As the headstone on the parents' grave was erected no earlier than 1953, approximately 37 years after the soldier's death, the one month error is understandable.

Private Ashcroft is interred at Grave Reference 1121 B 14 Douchy - Les Ayette British Cemetery, Pas de Calais, France. The village lies approximately 14 kilometres south of Arras on the road to Amiens. As the village was occupied by the Germans from October 1914 to March 1917 it is assumed his mortal remains were interred in this cemetery after 1917.

Upper left is a photograph of JOHN HENRY JONES the younger brother of Frank.

John was an under age volunteer, who enlisted when he was 17 years old. Like so many of the younger men he would serve his country again. The photograph taken circa 1940 shows him in his World War 2 uniform.

Lower left photograph is of FRANK JONES the son of Benjamin and Esther Jones who resided at 2 Stamford Road (now Willaston Road), Moreton.

Both photographs are provided courtesy of Mrs Barbara Jones.

THOMAS WARING

PRIVATE 20196 7(SERVICE) KINGS OWN SCOTTISH BORDERERS

Thomas H Waring was born in Moreton. The only son of Margaret and Thomas Waring. The father was a man of many talents, as he was the local undertaker, builder, plumber and wheelwright. The Waring's postal address was simply Main Road, the house is now number 162 Hoylake Road.

In May 1915 young Tom Waring and two of his pals, namely Bob Hale and Roy Borrowman, set off to join the Kings Own Scottish Borderers (KOSB). In order to join the colours, the lads travelled to Birkenshaw in Yorkshire. Decades later the reason for the long journey is not known. A popular theory however is that many volunteers made similar long journeys simply for the adventure of an express train journey. Travel outside of the volunteer's home district was still a novel experience. The three pals were all under military age but despite this they were drafted into the regiment. Some time later Bob Hale returned home. This was possibly due to parental intervention regarding their under age volunteer. Young lads often enlisted under an alias, in an attempt to avoid this type of parental intervention. The remaining two Moreton lads continued their training for the front. After less than four months' training the chums were separated, Roy Borrowman being despatched to Gallipoli, Private Tom Waring served with the 7/KOSB, the original battalion was posted to France and Flanders in early July 1915. Some time later Private Tom Waring followed these men abroad, as a casualty replacement. Less than a year after volunteering Corporal Waring was killed in action on 11th May 1916. The Corporal was only nineteen years of age.

On the day of his death the Kosbies were serving in the Loos sector South of the German stronghold, the Hohenzollern Redoubt. The KOSB position was known as"The kink" due to a pronounced kink in the front line trench. This position was notorious for sniping, hostile mining and tunnelling activity. There was also plenty of artillery bombardments. On 11th May a fierce artillery barrage descended along the divisional front, commencing in the morning and lasting all day. Shortly before six in the evening, the artillery altered their bombardment to a box barrage. This form of intense barrage exists when the guns which had been bombarding targets along the length of the front line, all concentrate their immense firepower on a small area. Shortly after, the enemy attacked and captured the pulverised trench system. Counter attacks were made to regain the kink sector, with only slight success. Ever-rising casualty figures later resulted in a merger of the 7th and 8th Battalions.

Located in the Pas de Calais (an administrative area similar to our counties) lies the village of Vermelles which lies midway between Bethune and Lens, to the north of the main road connecting these towns. On the south western outskirts of the village lies the neat Vermelles British Cemetery. The final resting place of Corporal Thomas Waring lies at grave reference III G 5.

The flow of volunteers began to steadily decrease at a time when every available man was desperately needed, stringent measures were now required if victory was to be assured. On 4/1/16 Mr Asquith, the Prime Minister introduced in the Commons a bill for compulsory military service, which excluded Ireland, all other United Kingdom males and widowers aged between 18 - 41 without dependant children were to be conscripted. The last day for single men to volunteer was 2/3/16, none of the conscripts served overseas before 1917. Failure to register for service meant a date would be appointed five weeks after the passing of the bill after which the conscript would be required to enlist for the duration of the war. Exemptions were granted to those medically unfit, sole wage earners or persons engaged in war production. Any conscientious objectors were assigned to non-combatant roles. These could range from a comfortable posting to the extremely hazardous role of a stretcher bearer on a shell swept battlefield. On 4/3/1916 the first call on single attested men was made, followed swiftly by the call-up of married men. The failure to register inevitably led to a court appearance in July the Wirral Tribunal had before them a Moreton man. The conscientious objector declared his refusal to take up arms against Germany, stating he bore the aggressor no malice. The Tribunal was unimpressed by the defendant's argument, the Judge describing the man as an amateur objector who presented the wrong case for his defence. The Judge stated that had the man pleaded an exemption on the grounds of caring for his disabled father he would have been exempted from military service.

Regardless of the global strife, life on the home front continued more or less as usual. In late April a vestry meeting discussed the Christ Church yearly accounts. There appears to have been a journalist covering this tedious meeting who reported that a Roll of Honour had been skilfully drawn up for the Parish by Mr

R Hughes, comprising of 96 names. An Easter card was also forwarded to each of these servicemen. The Easter church service and communion was also dedicated to them. Unfortunately the fate of this particular Roll of Honour is unknown. The Rectory which stood on the left side of Christ church (Shown below), was demolished in 1922 when most of the redundant or obsolete church records appear to have been disposed of.

While this book deals predominately with khaki clad soldiers it should also be remembered that the Royal Navy saw action throughout the globe. The greatest Naval engagement of the war occurred on 31st May when the Royal and Imperial German Navy clashed at Jutland, off the Danish coast. Both sides suffered serious losses and severe casualties; the sea battle produced no clear victor. On June 5th the Secretary of State for War, Lord Kitchener was outward bound for Russia on board HMS Hampshire. While off the Orkneys the vessel struck a mine and sank with only 12 survivors. Lloyd George took over the position of the late Lord Kitchener.

The menace of the Zeppelin and the increasing use of bomber aircraft ensured the national blackout continued. Although this area received no hostile ariel or naval attacks the blackout was still rigidly adhered to. In mid July Moreton man Joseph William Bell was charged with showing a light. The maximum fine for this transgression was £100.

HERBERT GARDNER SMITH

PRIVATE   W/731   13 (SERVICE) CHESHIRES

Bert Smith was born in Saughall Massie, the eldest son of Annie and Samuel Smith. His parents were tenants of Carr Gate Farm, Saughall Massie, which had been in the family for generations. The farm stood at the junction of Carr Lane and Hoylake Road. Many of the local lads were keen amateur musicians and Bert Smith was said to be a popular violinist. Young Bert Smith was a cousin of Percy Smith, both families being related to the Stanley family.

In September 1914 the young farm worker volunteered to fight the Hun and joined the 13th battalion of the Cheshire Regiment. The regiment was raised at Port Sunlight and had the unofficial title of "The Wirral Pals". After undergoing a year's training the New Army battalion of Kitchener's volunteers embarked on the SS Victoria, the vessel sailing for war-torn France on 24th September 1915.

Private H G Smith served as a Signaller with 3 company. After nine months at the front the battalion were active in the Douave Valley, near Mont St Eloi, which is south west of Vimy Ridge, France. In an attempt to by-pass the machine guns which swept the terrain with their murderous fire, a new tactic was employed. Warfare in selected areas became subterranean. Specialist mining companies were formed. One such group were excavating Liverpool's sewers and three days later they were Sappers digging mine shafts in France. The mine tunnels extended under the opposition's front line trenches, the mine heads being packed with tons of explosives. At zero hour the mines were detonated blasting the enemy to oblivion. Each side then raced to occupy the forward face of the crater.

In the days preceding Private Smith's untimely demise the battalion's war diary entry for 15/5/1916 records that *"At 8.30 pm the allies sprang mines and occupied the near lips. The enemy attacked at two locations placing a very heavy barrage on our trenches and advanced. At the same time the enemy made a strong attack on our lip of the crater. The attacking force assaulted the flanks and also came directly across the crater. This attack was repeated and continual attempts were made by the enemy to bomb (Mills bombs were an early form of hand grenade) us from our position. All attempts were beaten back with loss to the enemy. The trench fighting became critical by 10.30 pm due to a shortage of bombs. Two men were sent back repeatedly under heavy fire to obtain bombs. The dire situation was resolved by the arrival of the Royal Irish Rifles who brought up two hundred bombs. By 11.15 pm the bombing attacks ceased."*

The following day the weather was fine and the battalion was in the support trenches. Hostile aeroplanes flew over our lines from the south at 7.45 am. We further consolidated the lip of our crater. The firing of our eighteen pounders was excellent, as they just cleared the lip of our crater. The casualties of the previous night were detailed as - killed other ranks 12, wounded other ranks 34.

On Wednesday 17/5/1916 the battalion were again in support. Weather was fair. Enemy artillery and trench mortars were active all day. Casualties were reported as 4 other ranks wounded. Attention was drawn to the fact that W/208 L/Cpl W T Dodd and W/731 Private Herbert Smith had died of wounds.

While the war diarist reported the death of twenty years old Signaller H G Smith, he actually died at a Casualty Clearing Station (CCS) approximately 15 kilometres away. The fatally wounded soldier's family received a letter of sympathy from his nurse who described the soldier's bravery and cheerfulness. According to his nephew, Private Smith had lost his hand as the result of an explosion.

Private Smith is interred at Aubigny Communical Cemetery Extension, Pas de Calais, France. The grave reference is IB55. Aubigny-en-Artois is a village 15 kilometres north west of Arras. The poignant legacy of the 42nd, 30th, 24th and 1st Canadian CCS remains as a neat war graves cemetery, which adjoins the local cemetery.

This is the commemorative plaque issued to the next of kin of Herbert Smith

This had been provided courtesy of Mr C Smith and his brother.

On 26/2/1916 the Germans launched an attack on the French defences north-east of Verdun. For long desperate months the encircled troops in the Verdun sector repulsed most of the attacks. The German's attempt to literally bleed the French Army dry failed. It did, however, put immense pressure on the British to mount a massive attack to relieve the pressure on the beleaguered defenders of Verdun. Political intrigue and mistrust amongst the Allies determined the location for the battle. The two Nations' Armies overlapped in the Somme sector producing an arena for an offensive side by side. The Somme which had previously been a relatively quiet sector now witnessed the months of build-up of men, munitions and field hospitals, etc. A week long preliminary bombardment intended to destroy the enemy ceased on 1st July, the 132nd day of the siege of Verdun. The cream of Kitchener's Army rose from the trenches at 0730 hours 14 British Divisions boldly advanced across No Mans Land. They had repeatedly been assured the Hun would have been obliterated and the enemy barbed wire would have been cut to shreds. Yet the Germans had survived and emerged practically unscathed from their subterranean bunkers carved out forty feet below the surface. They quickly set up their machine guns then proceeded to scythe down the advancing waves of men as they advanced towards the uncut wire. The first day of the Somme produced modest gains, the Butchers Bill stood at 57,470 British casualties, comprising of 19,240 killed and 35,493 wounded. It is estimated that within the first ten minutes of the "Big Push" the British Army sustained 14,000 dead. The British were to continue attacks on the Somme for a further 142 days, exacting a terrible retribution for their fallen comrades.

A 1913 photograph of Drummer Arthur Stanley of the Cheshire Regiment

Photograph provided courtesy of Mrs P Hoare.

Arthur Stanley was wounded and buried alive by a shell explosion in July 1916. The trauma resulted in a medical discharge due to severe shell shock, a condition which persisted for several years.

HERBERT BOSTOCK

SERGEANT   12483   9 (SERVICE) CHESHIRE REGIMENT

Herbert Bostock was born in St Pauls parish district of Birkenhead. His parents were Jesse and Robert Bostock, who had an additional three sons and daughters. The father of this family was for many years the Chief Baker to the Pacific Steam Navigation Company. The family resided at "Stone House" which still faces Leasowe Common. During the war years the family moved to a large new bungalow in Pinetree Grove, Moreton.

Herbert Bostock was employed by Birkenhead Corporation at Woodside, the Birkenhead Ferry terminal, where for seventeen years he was employed as a Goods Clerk. He was described as a single man with an amiable disposition, a keen cyclist and a member of the cycling club. He was a National Reservist who joined the Cheshire Regiment immediately war was declared. He served as a Lance Sergeant! in the newly formed 9th battalion of the Cheshire Regiment, which arrived in France on the 19th June 1915.

At the Battle of Loos (25th September - 8 October) the 9th and 11th battalions were the first New Army battalions of the Cheshires to make their appearance under fire. The 9th originally served in the 58th Brigade of the 19th Division. On 25th September they helped reinforce the attack of the Welsh Regiment, but the attack was held up by belts of uncut wire and machine gun fire. The following year the battalion was engaged in the infamous Battle of the Somme. On the 1st of July the battalion, now a part of the 58th Brigade was in reserve for the attack on La Boiselle, which was a comparative failure. The Brigade containing the 9/Cheshires was ordered to attack at 10.30 pm that evening. The 9th battalion was in the line near Lochnagar, and encountered great difficulty advancing as the trench system was crammed full of dead and wounded soldiers. Prior to the morning's attack a huge mine was sprung under the German front line. British survivors of the morning attack were still holding the crater, also a part of the German line. The 9th battalion now assisted in holding the line. The following morning at 4.30 the battalion went over the top and charged forward. The advance was held up by a deep and wide trench, bombers were sent in either direction to clear a route through the maze of trenches. To attack across the surface of the battlefield would have been suicidal due to the machine guns and deep belts of uncut wire, the only option being fierce trench fighting. Despite all their efforts by the 3rd July the battalion was still three hundred yards away from La Boiselle, and after another day's vicious fighting the battalion was relieved.

During one of these actions Sergeant Bostock sustained gunshot wounds to the abdomen. He was invalided back to Blighty where he was taken to Stockport Western General Hospital. The thirty-one year old soldier died in hospital on 22nd August 1916.

The funeral cortege of the late Herbert Bostock departed from 17 Alverstone Road, Birkenhead. The coffin was draped with the Union Flag and at the head of the cortege was a detachment of the Cheshire Regiment. The internment service was at Flaybrick Cemetery, Birkenhead. A squad of Cheshires under the command of Sergeant Duckworth fired three volleys over the graveside and the service was concluded by the sounding of the Last Post. Sergeant Bostock's grave lies next to his parents' grave. The grave reference 4.8 bearing a Commonwealth War Graves Commission headstone is located in the Church of England section near the ruins of the derelict chapel.

The 11/Cheshires whose progress we have closely followed also fought on the Somme. They formed a part of the 75th Brigade of the 25th Division, which had one Cheshire battalion in each Brigade. They arrived on the Somme the day before the "Big Push", the 11th went into battle on 3rd July. The forthcoming attack was flawed due to an eleventh hour change of plan, the customary loss of communications and trenches packed with wounded setting the scene for disaster. The dire situation was compounded by a direct hit on the Brigade H.Q. effectively wiping out the command structure. The waiting Cheshires saw the 8/

Borders advancing and joined the attack, which had only minimal artillery support. They were faced with a withering fire of machine gun bullets, under which they walked forward till the battalion melted away. The Colonel was killed and every Company Commander was a casualty. At roll call from the 20 Officers and 657 men who took part in the attack only 6 Officers and 50 men remained.

ALEXANDER MALLOCK WILSON

L/CORPORAL 4500 2/SOUTH AFRICAN INFANTRY

Alexander M Wilson was the second son of John and Helen Williams. The family originally resided at 41 Leece Street, Liverpool before moving to the Wirral. The family then lived in "Glebelands" Upton Road, Moreton. Alexander emigrated to Durban, South Africa where he practised as an accountant. He married Mary Ferguson Taylor, the marital home was at 445 Innes Road, Durban, Natal.

On 19/8/15 the thirty year old was taken on the strength of the 2/South African Infantry (Natal and Orange Freestate battalion). On 6/5/16 he was promoted to Unpaid Lance Corporal, serving with B Company. The South African's baptism of fire was to be on the Somme.

Seven miles from the town of Albert lies the village of Longueval and the infamous Delville Wood. The 150 acre wood commanded the high ground, which made the wood of strategic importance. The Germans had held both objectives for two years; during this period both locations were heavily fortified. A fortnight after the commencement of the Battle of the Somme, more correctly known as the first battle of Albert, the 9th Scottish Division captured Longueval on the 14th July. The South African Brigade was then ordered to take Delville (Devils) Wood. This was the Springboks first engagement, death and glory now beckoned. At sunrise on 15th July the attack commenced, every yard of the South Africans' advance being fiercely contested by the entrenched foe. Desperate hand to hand fighting raged for days, until eventually the majority of the Germans were cleared from most of the wood. The victory proved to be short lived. On 18th July the German artillery pulverised the wood for over seven hours. Within two hours the oak and birch wood was obliterated, the German rate of artillery fire has since been calculated at over 400 shells a minute. When the bombardment finally ceased a massed assualt overwhelmed the beleaguered Empire troops. Heroic actions were fought amidst the shattered tree stumps, water filled shell holes and corpses of friend and foe. The allies fell back and regrouped, the Hun attack was halted by concentrated machine gun and artillery fire.

The remnants of the South African Brigade were relieved on 20th July. At roll call, from the 3,153 Springboks who entered the wood only 780 survivors remained. The entire wood was taken by the 38th Welsh Division on August 28th 1918.

Lance Corporal Wilson was killed in action at Delville Wood on the 18th of July. He has no known grave and for this reason his name is recorded on the massive Thiepval Memorial to the missing. The huge monument which dominates the Somme battlefield records a staggering 73,412 names, including Lance Corporal Wilsons' which is etched on pier and face 4C. The memorial can be found on the D73, off the main Bapaume to Albert Road,the D929.

Closer to home the noble sacrifice of the Wilson brothers is recorded on the plinth of their parents' memorial stone at Christ Church. The date of Alexander's death is recorded as the 14th, this is incorrect. The Moreton war memorial also refers to his service with the South African Regiment, an easy error which has also proven incorrect. The bereaved family were obviously supplied with incorrect information. Extensive research through a variety of reference sources have confirmed the errors.

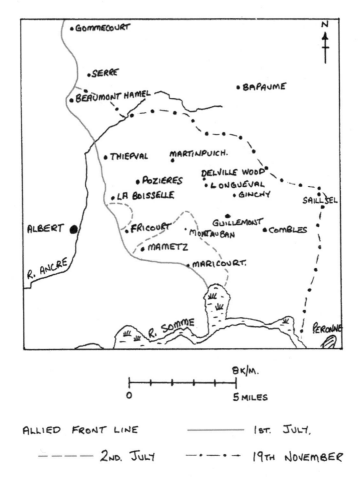

THE BATTLE OF THE SOMME

July to November 1916

ERNEST HARDCASTLE

PRIVATE   G/16345   9(SERVICE) CHESHIRE REGIMENT

Ernest was one of three sons to William and Mary Hardcastle, who were long standing Moreton residents. They also had two other sons, Oswald and Thomas. Prior to the war Ernest resided with his Grandmother, Mrs T Richards, at the farm house which was located at the junction of Digg Lane and Hoylake Road. In civilian life Ernest was employed by Mr Thomas the Moreton Baker. The three brothers volunteered for military service upon the outbreak of hostilities.

Private Hardcastle served with the newly formed 9th Battalion of the Cheshires. The battalion first saw action at Loos, the survivors considered this was good experience which would stand them well in the future "Big Push". The battalion was spared the tragic zero hour attack on the first day of the Somme, as they were held in reserve to the costly attack at La Boiselle. Private Hardcastle would have been in the same action as the previously mentioned Sergeant Bostock. Following the action at La Boiselle the 9/Cheshires were granted an all too brief relief period, enabling the depleted battalion to be brought up to strength with fresh drafts of men. Once again the Cheshires immersed themselves in battle, constantly being pitched against the fortified bastions straddling the Somme. The battalion withdrew from the trenches on August 1st. They were located near the town of Albert. The following days were spent on the move, returning to the trenches on 9th August at map location, York House.

On September 1st the battalion spent a few days at Butterfly Camp. This preceded moves to Lochre and Papot, before returning to the trenches on the 8th day. On the 14th September the 9/Cheshires were at Pont de Nieppe, close to the outskirts of Armentieres. The town is close to the Belgian-French border and was alternatively occupied by both sides. Due to its proximity to the trenches, the British Army used it as a forward base and it became popular with the Tommies as a recreation area.

The gathering of intelligence regarding the enemy's strength and weaknesses is an important factor in warfare. One of the methods used during this war was to raid an enemy trench, capture prisoners and return the captives to base for

81

interrogation. On paper the task appeared simple but in reality the infantry dreaded these raids which they considered as suicidal. Such trench raids often produced proportionately high casualties amongst the small party. On the night of 15/16th September a small group of 9/Cheshires were involved in a Commando type raid on the enemy trenches. Despite penetrating the enemy defences the raiders were repulsed, and the mission was considered a failure. The survivors did however manage to return with maps and paperwork. As expected the casulties were high. They sustained, 3 Junior Officers wounded, 3 other ranks killed, 12 other ranks wounded (it is assumed Pte Ernest Hardcastle was one of these men) and two others missing believed killed. The 22 year old Moreton soldier died of his wounds on 16th September 1916. At about this time his two brothers were reported as being in hospital recovering from wounds.

Private Ernest Hardcastle is interred within London Rifle Brigade Cemetery, Belgium. The grave reference number is 11 D 16. The cemetery is located 15 kilometres south of Ypres (Ieper), on a road which connects Ieper with Wijtschate, Mesen and Ploegsteert. The cemtery lies 800 metres beyond the village of Ploegsteert.

Wallasey Battalion at Moreton

The Wallasey Battalion is to camp at Moreton on Saturday and Sunday 23rd and 24th September. They are to meet at the Battalion Headquarters on Saturday. Great coats and haversacks are to be worn. Brassards must be worn by any volunteers without uniform. The band, drums and bugles, ambulance department, signallers and transports section are to attend. The following articles should be packed, a canvas or similar bag, carefully labelled with the special label provided through OC companies and left at Headquarters not later than twelve noon on Sunday 23rd instant. Two blankets, soap, towel, shaving materials and other necessaries not exceeding in the total twenty pounds. The charge per head will be four shillings, procuring three meals and billet but exclusive of any railway fare.

The above notice from the 16th September 1916 edition of the Wallasey News relates to the 11 (Wallasey) battalion of the Cheshire Volunteer Regiment. This part-time Home Defence force was the Home Guard of its day, and was based at the rear of the now demolished Liscard Fire Station at Manor Road. This battalion and the Birkenhead territorials were frequent visitors to Leasowe Common. This could be the attributing factor as to why the initial draft of Moreton men preferred the 11/Service battalion of their county regiment. The flat terrain of Leasowe Common proved an ideal training ground, with the benefit of good camping facilities. In bygone times a rifle range existed on the shore side corner of Leasowe and Pasture Road but the range fell into disuse and is not shown on a map of 1912. Occasionally lead musket balls have been discovered on the site. During the first world war a rifle range and trenches existed in the vicinity of Leasowe Castle, to the annoyance of the local authorities these were constantly damaged by people crossing to the sandhills.

PERCY SMITH

PRIVATE   24478   11 (SERVICE) CHESHIRE REGIMENT

Percy was the son of John George and Martha Smith. The farming family worked and resided at Carr Farm, Saughall Massie. Percy was a cousin of the earlier mentioned Private H G Smith. Percy was one of the Argyle Theatre volunteers who joined up in late January 1915. The soldier would later witness the gradual erosion of the original battalion and the steady influx of fresh drafts as the New Army battalions which had taken two years to raise and train were ripped apart on the Somme.

The opening days of October 1916 saw the 11/Cheshires still involved on the Somme killing fields. On the 6th October whilst under the cover of darkness the battalion was relieved in the line by the Lancashire Fusiliers. As the Cheshires filed out of the line many would have been counting their blessings. The forty eight hour stretch of trench duty had resulted in the loss of 2 O/Rs killed and 14 wounded. The following day at Aveluy 400 men of the battalion managed to have a long awaited bath. The following days were spent digging trenches and carrying supplies.

On the 10th October the battalion was located at "Ovillers Post". The village of Ovillers lies approximately midway between the town of Albert and the village of Thiepval. Ovillers itself was stormed on the 1st July but did not fall until the 16th. At 7 pm on October 10th a working party of 180 strong under the command of 2/Lt G E Barton was despatched to dig "New Bainbridge" fire trench. These trenches were parallel to the enemy trench system, the forward side of the trench had a firestep for the riflemen to fire from. The nocturnal activities of the Cheshires alerted the Germans, who rapidly brought their machine guns to bear and enfiladed the working party. The British who were caught in the open, sustained the following casualties the 2/Lt was wounded, 3 O/Rs killed and a further 14 wounded.

The battalion were involved in further digging and carrying parties on the 11th and 12th, prior to coming out of the line unscathed on 13th October. All the evidence points to Private Percy Smith being wounded on the night of 10th October. The Saughall Massie soldier was then evacuated probably by hospital train a distance of 90 miles to the town of Rouen. A vast military hospital complex sprawled around the southern outskirts of Rouen, the area contained 15 various hospitals and one convalescent depot. Within this complex Private Percy Smith succumbed to his mortal wounds, passing from this world on 13/10/1916. The mortal remains of the 22 years old man are interred at grave reference B.14.30 in St Sever Cemetery and Extension. This is located about 3 kilometres south of Rouen Cathedral and a short distance west of the road from Rouen to Elbeuf.

The inclusion of Carr in many of the farm names is derived from Kjarr a verb originally used to describe a marsh. The Carr area today is usually referred to as Meols.

GEORGE PARKINSON

PRIVATE   39802   2/ROYAL WELSH FUSILIERS

George Parkinson was born in Moreton. He was the third son of John and Elizabeth, who resided at Lemington House, Moreton. John's occupation is recorded as a farmer at Church Farm on Upton Road. At an unknown date George enlisted into the Army at Birkenhead.

The 2nd battalion originally consisted of regular soldiers arrived in France in late August 1914. By the beginning of November 1916 the 2/R.W.F. were still embroiled in the shell pocked, quagmire of the Somme battlefield. The Somme offensive had now dragged on for five bloody months. The slaughter of a generation continued during the Battle of Ancre Heights, a costly assault fought during the period 3 - 7th November 1916. The 33rd Infantry Division played a significant role in the battle. The Division contained thirteen battalions, including the 2/ R.W.F. On 3rd November the battalion entered the line at Les Boeufs. The day's casualties consisted of 4 O/Rs killed, 8 O/Rs wounded and 3 missing. The following day heavy hostile shelling occurred between 4.30 to 5.15, the barrage gradually decreasing during the remainder of the day. Casualties were 1 O/R killed, 5 O/Rs wounded and 4 missing. On the eve of the planned offensive an Officer led 30 men from B Company in a night time raid on a strategic German position. The raid was unsuccessful the Fusiliers incurring severe casualties. On Sunday 5th November at 11.10 am the Division advanced across the quagmire of rain filled shell holes. The enemy machine guns were still the undisputed kings of the battle field. The 2/R.W.F. advanced under a protective artillery barrage close on the heels of the retiring Hun. By noon the 2/R.W.F. were digging in 100 yards short of their original objective. The trench digging continued all night. The battalion's casualties were 2 officers wounded, 19 O/Rs killed, 54 O/Rs wounded and 10 missing. Trench digging continued the following day, resulting in 5 O/Rs killed and 3 O/Rs wounded. The following 24 hours entailed even more digging under sporadic fire, claiming further lives. Casualties were 1 Officer wounded, 7 O/Rs wounded, 10 O/Rs missing. The remnants of the battalion were relieved by the 1/ Devons on the night of the 6th. No further casualties were incurred during the remainder of November.

No doubt Private Parkinson was mortally wounded during the Battle of Ancre Heights. He was evacuated by rail to the 36th Casualty Clearing Station at Mericourt l'Abbe, Somme where he died on 12th November 1916. A stark reminder of the C.C.S. is Heilly Station Cemetery, where Private G Parkinson is interred at grave reference V.E.12. The village of Mericourt l'Abbe lies approximately 19 kilometres north east of Amiens and 10 kilometres south west of Albert. Heilly Station Cemetery is about 2 kilometres south west of Mericourt l'Abbe on the south side of the road to Corbie.

The death of 20 years old Private Parkinson is recorded on a headstone at Christ Church. His self-sacrifice is also recorded on the neighbouring village of Bidston's war memorial.

While the previous pages are mainly concerned with the local men who died for their country, it should be remembered scores of local men survived the carnage - their exploits remain unrecorded - now lost for ever. Most of the local men served with the Cheshire Regiment, which deployed the 1st, 5th, 6th, 9th 10th, 11th 13th 15th and 16th battalions on the Somme.

On 15th September the first tanks rumbled into action on the Somme. However insufficient numbers were available to deliver a knockout punch. The impetus was in the main wasted, although in some areas the Germans fled in terror as the iron mastodons approached. The Somme battles gradually ceased during November like two exhausted and battered prize fighters they had fought themselves to a standstill. The high casualties of the Somme battles were originally concealed from the British public, many of whom thought their loved ones were Prisoners of War. The atrocious casualty figures were gradually released to the press in a manner which attempted to maintain morale. Their efforts were belied by the returning wounded veterans who told of the utter carnage. The concentrated local recruiting of the Pals' battalions now produced whole towns in mourning for their dead, slaughtered en masse on the Somme. An ever-increasing amount of households now received the dreaded telegram stating *"It is my sad duty to inform you of ....."*. The Prime Minister experienced the nation's grief when his son was also killed on the Somme on 15th September.

By now the conditions on the Somme were appalling, the fragile earth which had died a thousand deaths, surrendered to the destructive forces of modern warfare. Pleasant countryside, littered with idyllic ponds and ancient woodland, was replaced with a churned and blasted wasteland devoid of landmarks. The continual artillery bombardments annihilated the countryside's natural drainage system and by early Winter the land was a morass of thick mud. The persistent rain combined with the thawing of the first snows turned the battlefield into a swamp. Thus it was that the weather rather than the Generals closed the curtain on the Somme offensive. On both sides the "poor bloody infantry" prepared for another arduous winter in the line of trenches, scattered throughout the lunar-like landscape of utter desolation.

The estimated casualties of men killed, wounded, prisoner-of-war, and missing on the Somme up to November 1916 are calculated as - British 420,000, French 204,000 and German 670,000. The allies gained a thirty mile strip of territory which had a maximum width of only 7 miles. Winston Churchill wrote *"The actual battle fronts were not appreicably altered - no strategic advantage of any kind has been gained"*. The Somme campaign unnerved the politicians, several of whom were now calling for a peace settlement without victory. By November the political situation was acute, the beginning of December bringing about the resignation of Mr Asquith. The new Premier Mr Lloyd George formed a new National government, dedicated to victory. On 18th December the French Army's defence of Verdun successfully concluded, the Somme attacks having successfully prevented the vanquished Germans from transferring men to Verdun.

Don't be Alarmed,
the Cheshires are on guard

Unlike the previous years this was to be a year of victories enabling the Allies to gradually advance and in February a total of 11 fortified villages and 2,169 prisoners were taken.The Nation's hopes soared with the realisation that the entrenched Hun was not invincible and was now tasting defeat. This buoyed the civilians' spirits at a time when the cost of food had risen by 100%. Most wages had increased but only by approximately 40%. The enemy U-boats were sinking an alarming amount of cargo vessels laden with war materials and food. By Spring food shortages were evident and the weekly meat ration was reduced to ¾lb. Although a war tax had been levied on tea, this was now rationed as was butter. The Germans endured a far worse scenario due to the Royal Navy blockade. On the Western Front the Germans began to fall back to a new fortified zone known as the Siegfried Stellung, referred to by the British as the Hindenberg Line.

Throughout the war the authorities ensured Leasowe Castle was utilised for several purposes. By this time it was serving as a Military Convalescence Depot for wounded veterans. A tragedy occurred there in February when 43 year old Sgt Alfred Birch of the Cheshire Regiment, choked to death after having had a hearty meal.

Throughout this unsettled period, life within the self-sufficient villages of Moreton and Saughall Massie managed to retain an air of normality. Yet for the tenant farmers agricultural life became more arduous than usual. The prospect of food shortages now necessitated even higher levels of food production, despite a shortage of experienced farm labour. An influx of inexperienced "Townie" farm hands severely tried the farmers' patience who often resented the substitute for "our Jack" out in France. The introduction of conscription effectively stripped the land of any fit young man of military age. An indication of the predicament facing the farmers was revealed in the local press. A Moreton farmer with 60 acres of land and eleven milking cows requested the Court for the exemption of an 18 year old youth, attested and in military group A. The young man was a wagoner and teamsman who assisted the farmer and a 15 year old boy on the farm; the trio supplied most of the farm labour. The farmer was assured that the youth would not be taken until a substitute had been found. To this the farmer replied "He hoped they would not send a French polisher", which provoked laughter.

After canvassing the local people the Reverend Spink established a patriotic War Savings Association within his Moreton parish. The Rev. R. L. Powell became Treasurer and the Chairman was

Rev. Spink who appears to have been an extremely busy man. During the vestry meeting held on Easter Monday, 9th April, he announced *"He was glad to have been able to prepare a new Roll of Honour containing the names of 132 men serving King and Country from the Parish"*. On the same day in France through sleet and snow the Battle of Arras was successfully launched across a 14 mile front. Amongst the gains, one of the most significant was the capture of Vimy Ridge by the Canadian Corps. Further good news was America had finally decided to enter the war, on the side of the allies.

The two following biographies are included because their deaths are recorded on a grave at Christ Church, Moreton.

HERBERT HENRY HARRIS

PRIVATE   48892   12 (SERVICE) KINGS LIVERPOOL

Herbert Henry Harris was the younger brother of Charles Russell Harris (see article). Their parents were Harriet and Jesse James Harris of 390 Park Road North, Birkenhead. Herbert was a married man who shared a home with his parents. The young man conducted a large window cleaning business based in the North End of Birkenhead for his father.

In September 1915 Herbert Harris went to Liverpool where he enlisted into the Kings Liverpool Regiment. The 12th battalion were raised at Seaforth the previous September, the original draft landed at Boulogne on 27th July 1915. At a later date Private

Harris would join the battalion in France, as a casualty replacement.

In mid-February 1917 the 12/Kings were camped at Carnoy. On the 19th February they were in the line near Morval, when the Germans launched a flammenwerfer (flame thrower) attack. The night offered no respite as the Bosche bombarded the line with lachrymatory (tear) gas shells, the bombardment being repeated the following morning. That night the Kingsmen were relieved; they had lost four other ranks killed, one officer and six other ranks wounded, while a further three other ranks were posted as missing presumed dead. The battalion retired to their billets at Camp 3 for a brief rest period. On February 25th the battalion re-entered the line returning to the same sector. Early on the morning of the 27th an intelligence gathering patrol entered the German trench system. The enemy discovered the intruders, the resulting skirmish was responsible for the deaths of a 2/Lt, 1 other rank killed and two more wounded. Trench life was uneventful until the 15th March when a tragic disaster occurred. The Kings were now at Camp 4, Carnoy. At 5.50 am, an old mine, which was positioned between the Officers' hut and the main camp, mysteriously exploded, demolishing the whole camp. The sleeping occupants of the huts were swiftly rescued. However, the disaster claimed the lives of 3 Officers, 9 other ranks and a further 52 other ranks were wounded.

The battalion war diary reports the Germans withdrew towards the Hindenburg Line on the night of the 17/18th. The retiring Hun operated a scorched earth policy, poisoning wells and destroying everything in their path. The 12/Kings were in billets at Guillemont. For the next four days they were detailed to clearing up the abandoned territory. On the 23rd they relocated to Le Transloy before moving to trenches east of Ytres on the 27th. Reconnaissance patrols discovered the village of Neuville was still occupied by the enemy. The village was attacked on the evening of the 28th. The battalion assembled at Battalion Headquarters, then at Bus, attacked with B and D companies reinforced with two sections of battalion bombers. The advancing 12/Kings endured intense machine gun fire, as they desperately struggled around three dense belts of barbed wire. Against the odds a toe hold was gained in Neuville, the battalions Lewis gunners and the battalions bombers, totally cleared the village by 2.30 am on the 29th March.

Private Harris died of wounds at the Base camp on 28.3.1917, probably as the result of the above action. The twenty year old is interred at grave reference I.D.19 Guards Cemetery, Combles, Somme. The small military cemetery is located 16.5 k/m east of Albert and 13k south of Bapaume. The young soldier's sacrificed life is recorded on the Birkenhead Cenotaph. The parents were now residing in Chapel Hill Road, Moreton. The death of their two sons is recorded on the family memorial stone at Christ Church.

The bereaved family were mourning the death of their loved one when fate dealt another cruel blow. Approximately five weeks after the death of Herbert the arrival of another telegram brougt the devastating news of the loss of another family member.

CHARLES RUSSELL HARRIS

PRIVATE   **243516**   **1/4 CHESHIRE REGIMENT**

Charles Russell Harris (brother of Herbert Henry) was born in Warrington, Cheshire. In later years he became the husband of Ethel Harris and the father of two children. The family resided at 6 Thornton Street, Birkenhead. Prior to army life he was employed in the dairy business and was well known in the North End of Birkenhead. Charles enlisted into the local territorial battalion on lst January 1917 his military training being carried out at Oswestry. Within a few months he was on a troopship, the S.S. Transylvania.

The one year old vessel was requisitioned from the Anchor Line in May 1915. The 567 foot long vessel was originally designed to carry 2,420 passengers in three classes. Her steam turbines drove twin propellers which gave the 14,315 gross tonnage vessel a top speed of sixteen knots. On 3rd May 1917 the British troop ship, escorted by the Japanese destroyers, Matsu and Sakaki, steamed from Marseilles outward bound for Alexandria. The manifest of the Transylvania records the vessel carried a cargo of general stores and troops. The overcrowded steamer was transporting 300 Officers, 2,800 other ranks, plus the ship's crew.

On 4th May 1917 the Transylvania steamed into the periscope sights of the U63. At approximately 10 am a German torpedo struck the troopship on the port side, exploding within the engine compartment. The Captain thought the vessel would probably stay afloat all day and might be towed into port. Despite this the lifeboats were lowered and life rafts thrown overboard. As the soldiers lined the decks prior to abandoning ship they sang to keep up their spirits. At the time of the explosion the two escorts were ¼ mile in front of the troopship; they now circled their wounded charge. The Matsu threw caution to the wind and came alongside the stricken vessel, which used a ship's boat to lower thirty men at a time onto the destroyer. Half an hour after the first torpedo another one came, unfortunately while a boat load of soldiers was being lowered. The destroyer crew saw the approaching torpedo and took evasive action, clearing the torpedo's trail by four feet. The torpedo missed its target which then hit the Transylvania exploding amidships, and blew the ship's boat and its human cargo to pieces. Men who had been thrown into the water were caught in the grip of the ship's propellers with deadly consequences. The S.S. Transylvania slid rapidly beneath the waves of the Gulf of Genoa, at a position of 44.15 North 08.30 East, which is approximately 2.5 miles south of Cape Vado. The survivors saw several ships pass by but their signals were not seen. Fortunately an Italian destroyer rescued them.

414 souls perished in this naval disaster and amongst the casualties was twenty-four year old Private Harris. The recovered bodies were afforded a full military funeral procession. Horse drawn wagons bearing the dead led a solemn procession of Naval and Army personnel through Savona. The mortal remains are interred in Savona Town Cemetery, Italy. The grave reference for Private Harris is C22. Charles is commemorated on his parents' headstone at Christ Church, Moreton. On 28th January 1924 Ethel Harris subscribed to the fund for the public financed Hamilton Square Cenotaph, which bears her deceased husband's name.

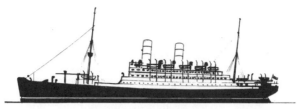

S. S. Transylvania

During the month of May the new German edict of unrestricted warfare on shipping was responsible for the sinking of 23 British, Allied and neutral vessels. Two further vessels were sunk by mines. In Flanders a two-part offensive was launched, the first attack objective was the Messines-Wytschaete Ridge south of Ypres. The capture of the ridge was imperative as it would enable the B.E.F. to break out of the Ypres salient. This would in turn enable the launch of the second phase against the Passchendaele-Staden Ridge. For the Messines attack the planning was meticulous, nothing being left to chance. Weeks of artillery bombardment would culminate in the detonation of nineteen mines planted beneath the German lines. At 3.10 am almost one million tons of high explosive blasted the Germans to oblivion. The dazed survivors were swiftly over-run by the allies. Despite pockets of fierce resistance by 9 am the ridge was in allied hands. Yet it would take months of costly fighting before the entire ridge dominating Ypres would at last belong to the allies.

DANIEL STANLEY

PRIVATE   24461   11(SERVICE) CHESHIRE REGIMENT

Daniel Stanley was one of the four sons of Elizabeth and James Stanley. The family were now residing at 3 Moreton Terrace, which was situated in Garden Lane, Moreton. The site of the small row of terrace houses is now a small car park. Prior to war service Dan Stanley was employed at a local market gardens. He was one of the original group of Moreton volunteers who volunteered in late January 1915. Private Stanley served with B Company of the 11th battalion of the Cheshire Regiment. During his brief service he had an alternative service number which was 22251.

Private Stanley would have seen action at Loos, the Somme, and Ancre Heights and was now preparing for the next action, the Battle of Messines. Numbered amongst the men of the 25th Division were four Cheshire battalions, which were under the command of the Anzacs - the Australian and New Zealand Army Corps. The Division was now in the Wulvergem sector of Flanders, and were to attack just North of Messines (now Mesen). On the 7th June 1917, Private Stanley and his comrades in the 11th battalion were in reserve in readiness for the 25th Division's attack on the Messines Ridge. At 6.50am the Cheshires left their assembly positions to attack the most distant of the Division's objectives. The artillery consisted of one gun for every seven yards of front. Advancing under the cover of concentrated artillery barrages, the 11th swiftly secured their objective. Spurred on by their success an Officer and some of the battalion found themselves attacking Despagne Farm. The Officer realised the party was ahead of the rolling barrage, the only option available was to shelter in shell holes and wait for the storm of steel and explosives. The bombardment fell in all its fury amidst them; fortunately most of the men managed to survive. The recently captured positions were rapidly consolidated, and supplied with all the materials necessary in readiness for a German counter attack. At 1.45pm a strong German counter attack emerged from the shallow banks of the Blauwepoort Beek which was a shallow stream. The attackers were beaten off by the 11th battalion and a platoon of the 8th Border Regiment. The timely intervention of boldy handled sections of machine guns was of great help.

The 11th Cheshires' attack on 7th June claimed the following casualties - 3 Officers and 43 other ranks killed, while a further 8 Officers and 170 other ranks were wounded. Amongst the dead was Private Stanley, a young man aged 23, cut down in the prime of life. The young warrior has no known grave, his self-sacrifice is recorded on the Menin Gate memorial to the missing at Ypres, Belgium.

The family were notified of their son's death on June 24th. A fortnight later a memorial service was held at Christ Church on Sunday 8th July.

MORETON'S SAD RECORD

FAMILY'S HEAVY BEREAVEMENT

Mr James Stanley, of 3 Moreton Terrace, Moreton has received the sad news that his son Pte Dan Stanley of the Cheshires, has been killed in action. Deceased was 23 years of age. Another son, Pte J Stanley of the Cheshires was wounded in November 1915 and died last November. He was aged 27 years. Drummer A Stanley, also of the Cheshires was wounded in July last, and was discharged owing to wounds, in October, as unfit for service. He was aged 23 years. Driver W Stanley of the Royal Field Artillery, 21 years old is still serving his country, and is now in Salonika. Out of 85 volunteers from the parish of Moreton who joined the colours in 1915, twelve have been killed and eighteen wounded and are still serving, whilst three have been discharged owing to wounds or loss of limb.

The above article is from the June 30th edition of the Birkenhead Advertiser.

William Ernest Knowles and family pose for the camera. The family portrait was taken at the rear of the garage which is between Manuden Villa and the Plough Inn.

This group photograph taken outside army hutments, was most likely taken at Park Hall Camp, Oswestry. Private Knowles is on the rear row, third from the left.

All kitted out in tropical kit ready for Mesopotamia. Private Knowles is shown in the rear row, second from left.

The three photographs of his Father are provided courtesy of Mr E Knowles.

WILLIAM ERNEST KNOWLES

ROYAL WELSH FUSILIERS

William Knowles and his family resided at "Manuden Villa" Moreton Park. The small house faces Sandbrook Lane, and is now a shop supplying the motor trade. When he was approximately 35 years of age, William left behind his young family and enlisted in the Army. He served with the Royal Welsh Fusiliers (R.W.F.). After completion of training Private Knowles and his comrades were due to depart for Mesopotamia (now Iraq). This indicates the Moreton soldier was with the 8 (Service) R.W.F. which departed to the Middle East in February 1916. Prior to her husband's departure overseas Mrs Knowles became seriously ill and this resulted in Private Knowles remaining within the United Kingdom. He then served in the Regimental Military Police, and the 1/4 Territorial battalion of the R.W.F. and in 1919 he was still serving in the Army.

(Photograph courtesy of the Mitchell family)

Three members of the Clarke family who resided at Moreton
Terrace, Garden Lane served King and Country. The above
photograph is of Private Harold Clarke. Although his Kings
Liverpool Regiment cap badge is clearly visible he is thought to
have been one of the Liverpool Pals. Lord Derby presented each
of the original Liverpool Pals with their own unique sterling silver
cap badge. These much sought after badges were frequently
stolen by members of rival regiments, resulting in Pals wearing
the less desirable line regiment cap badge. The photograph also
reveals other links with the Pals. According to Mrs V Beecroft, a
relative of Private Clarke, the Moreton soldier had a near escape
from the grim reaper. During a raid on an enemy trench system
Private Clarke was shot in the fingers and unable to fire his
rifle. He set off for the British lines but lost his way in the maze
of enemy trenches where he was confronted by a German.
Realising the wounded Tommy was no longer a threat, the
German soldier is reputed to have directed Harry Clarke towards
the British lines. As a result of his wounds the Moreton soldier
was invalided out of the army in 1917.

His brother, Private Thomas William Clarke (27418), served with the 1st Garrison battalion of the Cheshire Regiment. He departed for garrison duties at Gibraltar in September 1915.

ARTHUR GRAHAM BAIRD

ENGINEER   ROYAL NAVAL RESERVE

Arthur G Baird was the husband of Mrs Beatrice A Baird. The couple resided at "Fernleigh", Park Road, which is now known as 9 Knutsford Road, Moreton.

Junior Engineer Baird served with the Royal Naval Reserve, and with the exception of his final voyage on the S.S. Karina little is known about this man.

The 4,222 gross registered tonnage S.S. Karina was built in 1905 for the African Steamship Company. This was a subsidiary of Elder Dempster & Co. of Liverpool. The S.S. Karina left Sierra Leone, homeward bound laden with a cargo of palm oil and kernels. On 1st August 1917 the cargo boat was torpedoed by the U.C.75. The stricken vessel sank in the Atlantic at a position 17 miles, south, south west, 1.5 miles from Hook Point (3 miles south of Fethard, County Wexford). Amongst the 11 souls who perished was Arthur Graham Baird.

The death of the Engineer is commemorated on the St. Saviours' Church Memorial, Nigeria.

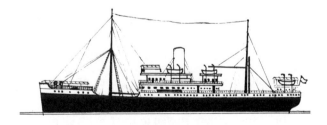

S. S. Karina

During the course of the conflict thousands of prisoners were taken captive by the opposing sides. The surrendered Germans were taken to Britain where they were dispersed amongst a network of Prisoner of War camps. Often the prisoners were expected to earn their keep, although they could refuse to work in war effort production. This resulted in thousands of internees working in agricultural or similar work. These men were utilised to replace the landworkers who had volunteered or been conscripted into the armed services. Within the County of Cheshire the allocation of enemy labour was administered by the Cheshire Agricultural Committee which was based at Crewe.

The Moreton area is predominately low-lying and is still prone to flooding in the Winter months. The area's surplus rainwater drains into the River Birkett and its tributaries, which in 1917 were in disrepair. The Engineer in charge of the Birkett renovation scheme successfully applied to the Cheshire Agricultural Committee for a workforce of German labour. In early September 140 German prisoners arrived as labour to clear the River Birkett and other watercourses. The prisoners and their armed escorts were housed at the nearby Leasowe Castle for almost the remainder of the war. Three weeks after work had commenced the Agricultural Committee made their first visit to inspect the scheme, which had begun close to Bidston railway junction and was gradually progressing towards Leasowe. By mid-August a distance of 1200 yards was cleared of years of accumulation of reeds, silt, etc., and proper banks were formed to prevent flooding. Shortly after the inspection an application for an extra 50 men with necessary guards was successfully applied for.

In Flanders the events at Ypres although never far from the headlines, once again dominated the newspapers. A fresh army initiative to burst out of the Ypres salient and simultaneously advance across the series of ridges encircling the town was about to be launched. The German defences in this area consisted of a network of concrete blockhouses which overlooked the surrounding terrain. Each pill box contained a machine gun sited in such a way as to provide a covering crossfire to its neighbour. Prior to the allied attack over 2,000 guns bombarded the enemy positions, and unknowingly they also destroyed the marshy ground's drainage system. On 31st July the infantry supported by tanks attacked and initially met with success. However the British attack stalled in the Gheluvelt plateau area, and at this crucial time it began to rain heavily. August transpired to be the wettest for years and turned the battlefield into a sea of thick mud, which literally bogged down the offensive. None-the-less the fighting continued throughout September and October and on 6th November the remains of the village of Passchendaele, near the northern extremity of the encircling ridge, finally fell to the Canadians.

PRIVATE JOHN B. G. GEORGE

One of the early casualties of the battle in the mud, officially known as Third Ypres was Private John B. G. George. He was the youngest son of Mr S. George who was the Leasowe Station Master; the family resided at Leasowe Station House. Once again the property has been demolished and is given over to traffic. John B. G. George attested on 17 November 1915 and served with the 1/10 battalion of the Liverpool Scottish. Originally the Leasowe soldier had the number 5676, which may have changed later to 356950. He went to France in April 1916, and appears to have been wounded during the fighting near the Ypres - Poperinghe road. After costly fighting the battalion was relieved on 3rd August, and the following day they departed on training exercises. The action had cost the Liverpool Territorials a total of 55 killed, 6 missing and 180 wounded. Amongst the latter was Private George who had received a gunshot wound in the left leg. Towards the end of August the Station Master's son was in a Manchester hospital receiving treatment.

The following may have been another reported casualty of the Flander's campaign. Private Percy Lindfield of Moreton and formerly Hoylake. In late August the Moreton soldier was reported as slightly wounded and brought to a hospital in Blighty. According to a family member the soldier sustained a thigh wound which had become infected by exposure to Mustard Gas. The wounded man's brother, Private Francis Lindfield, was also gassed some time during the conflict.

Undeterred by the carnage of Third Ypres the under-strength Allied force launched another attack, a fortnight after the capture of Passchendaele. New tactics were employed commencing on

20th November when almost 400 tanks spearheaded an assault on Cambrai. The surprise tactics produced a break-through several miles deep creating a salient within the Hindenburg Line. Unfortunately due to a lack of reserves the Allies were unable to capitalise on the breach. Strong German counter attacks supported by low flying ground attack aircraft, eventually captured most of the lost ground. Today there is no visible evidence that any Moreton men fought at Cambrai. If the locals were there they would have had an affinity with the tank "Birkenhead" which fought at Cambrai. During the attack on the village of Cantain on November 21st the "Birkenhead" was knocked out by a shell. She was repaired a few days later and was in action at Gouzeacourt, where she was badly scarred.

A cheery British Christmas card

If der 4th Cheshires
haf gone by, den I kan kom out.

The arrival of New Year was anything but happy for the freezing cold infantryman huddled in the dark bleak trenches. The battle weary guardians of the wasteland of trenches were now severely deficient in number. This came about due to the gradual annihilation of a generation of soldiers, the situation being further compounded by anxious politicians who introduced policies restricting the flow of potential cannon fodder to the front. Despite the manpower shortage Field Marshall Haig was confident the available resources could contain an enemy attack for eighteen days.

The German army had also endured appalling casualties, but their ranks were now swelled by the arrival of men and armaments transferred from the Eastern front. In the aftermath of the Russian Revolution, the Bolsheviks were no longer inclined to wage war against Germany, thus the Hun was now able to significantly bolster the Western Front force. The Central Powers confident of their numerical supremacy prepared for a Spring Offensive, which would crush the Allies before the American troops arrived en masse and upset the balance of military power. A knockout punch was essential as Germany was now in utter turmoil. The Royal Navy blockade not only kept a near muntinous German Navy bottled up in their home ports, it resulted in severe shortages of raw materials and foodstuffs. Extensive preparartions were now made for a Spring Offensive, a last ditch effort to turn the tide of the Great War in Germany's favour. The "Kaisers Battle" centred on the BEF was a bold attempt to force the weary troops back to the sea. If this force could be defeated the allies would collapse.

On March 21st at 4.40am code name Operation Michael commenced when almost 10,000 artillery pieces laid a thunderous earth shaking bombardment upon the Allies. The devastating blanket barrage of gas and explosive shells lasted several hours and succeeded in totally wiping out the allied infrastructure. When the barrage ceased the survivors manned their crumbling defences in readiness for the imminent infantry attack. The front line positions were cosseted in a blanket of thick fog out of which emerged an overwhelming German force. Spearheading this force were specially trained Stormtroopers whose lightening advance and tactical encirclement later became known as Blitzkreig. The opening stage of this great battle cost the allies 38,000 casualties of which 21,000 were taken prisoners of war. Germany suffered an even higher casualty rate. The allies withdrew before the advancing Germans, and by 23rd March some sections of the line were penetrated by almost 12 miles.

A grave at Christ Church records the sacrifice of Addison John Bousfield who was killed in action on 21st March 1918; he was aged 32. A J Bousfield was the son of Helena, a married man with at least one child. While the date of death coincides with the launch of Operation Michael, the author has been unable to discover any further information concerning this man. As his name is not recorded on either of the village memorials it is assumed he was not a local resident.

The desperate battles of 1918 produced the highest casualty rates of the war, the death rate being reflected within the Parish of Moreton which also experienced its blackest year. It is now assumed that the mortality rate would have been much less than the now unknown amount of local men captured, maimed and wounded. Eight decades later there are no local great war veterans left, to provide this information. In the face of battle the wounded crawled into shell holes which afforded meagre shelter from the guns. During the day the murderous conditions frequently prevented the arrival of basic medical assistance, the wounded usually lay on the battlefield until nightfall. In severe instances the isolated wounded men might lay for days in No Mans Land where their lives often ebbed away. Occasionally brave men risked their own lives in valiant attempts to rescue their fallen comrades. In the Spring of this year a Moreton soldier performed such a rescue.

George Richard Weston Davies was a former Welsh coal miner who relocated to Moreton prior to the outbreak of war. As the nearest coal face was approximately a dozen miles from Moreton, he worked locally as a building excavator. George later married one of the daughters of James Stanley.

Private Davies was an early volunteer for war service and was known to be on active service during November 1915, although not yet posted to France. The young volunteer was approximately 22 years old when he posed for the group photograph of the "Moreton Patriots". After several years of warfare his bravery in the field was officially acknowledged when the London Gazette edition of 28th March 1918 announced that Private G Davies 202524 of the Cheshire Regiment had been awarded the Distinguished Conduct Medal for conspicuous gallantry and devotion to duty. His citation for this relatively scarce gallantry award states the following:

> He went over the open ground under intense fire
> and brought in a wounded comrade to safety.
> He showed great gallantry and sacrifice.

It is assumed the incident occurred during the Spring Offensive. The award was later reported in the April edition of the Wallasey News.

Miraculously the "Moreton Patriots" survived the main thrust of "Operation Michael", but the smaller subsidiary attacks were to prove costly for the Moreton warriors. As ever the Somme battlefields continued to devour a generation, the totally destroyed villages which had been won at a terrific cost in young lives were now abandoned to the Germans. "Operation Georgette" or the "Lys Offensive" lasted from 9th April to the 29th and during this brief period Moreton lost more men than at any other period in the Great War. The month's events were categorised into several key battles each as strategically important as the other. Most of these titanic clashes claimed amongst the dead one of Moreton's finest.

GEORGE RICHARD EVAN LLOYDD

PRIVATE   359252   1/10 (SCOTTISH) KINGS LIVERPOOL

Ada Davidson Lloydd, a dressmaker. was the mother of the above soldier. At the beginning of the Great War, the mother's address was Leamington House, Upton Road, Moreton. The ground floor was converted to a shop, which for the past few decades has traded as Fosters fruit and vegetables. Upon Ada's death in 1935 and internment at Christ Church her son's sacrifice was recorded for posterity on her grave kerbstones; there is no longer a grave headstone. During the lengthy research period of this book the kerbstones have been unearthed and look destined for removal, no doubt for easier cemetery maintenance. The kerbstone states "George Richard Evan Lloydd, killed in action April 1918", which the author accepts as the true fact.

My research has revealed an anomaly concerning a Richard John Lloyd a fellow member of the Liverpool Scottish, who had the same regimental number. He is recorded as killed on the same day, and is also a Liverpool resident. This latter soldier appears to have no known grave and is not mentioned on any memorial to the missing, although unlike his namesake he does appear in Soldiers died in the Great War. Both of the soldiers are named in the Liverpool Scottish Roll Of Honour. The battalion's museum Curator admits errors do exist in the nominal role; it is therefore assumed both individuals are the same man. George Richard Evan Lloydd was born, lived and enlisted in Liverpool. He later became the husband of Edith May Lloydd, and they resided at 5 Stanmore Road, Wavertree, Liverpool. In the latter part of the conflict he attested to the Territorial battalion of the 1/10 Kings, serving as a Private soldier regimental number 359252.

On 9th April, Ludendorff launched the second phase of his offensive across the Lys valley, the attack occurred upon a 12 mile front from La Bassee to Armentieres. At 4.10am the enemy heavily bombarded all the trenches, artillery and rear positions of the Allied line with a combination of phosgene gas and high explosive shells. To help simplify matters the following passage recalls selective actions concerning the 55th Divisions, in particular the 1/10 Kings (Liverpool Scottish). The enemy penetrated the front line at a sector held by the Portugese, and as a result the left flank was exposed. The 1/10 Kings who had been in reserve at Le Hamel dispersed to their battle positions, in doing so they sustained heavy casualties from shell fire. They occupied a vacated section of the line and assisted in holding the vital left flank. The shelling subsided by evening, and the night was spent reinforcing the shell battered positions. The following day at dawn the attacks recommenced, in the main they were repulsed. In one attack a 60 strong enemy raiding party by- passed a front line trench by wading along a ditch; the alarm was raised by a Cook. A company each of the 1/5 South Lancs and 1/10 Kings engaged the enemy in hand to hand fighting successfully repelling the foe. On the 11th the Territorial's position was targeted by a field gun firing at point blank range, causing frequent casualties. Throughout the day scores of counter attacks were launched in valiant attempts to regain the old British line. On the night of 11/12th a company each of the 1/10 and 13th Kings successfully recaptured a key position known as "The Keep" and eliminated an enemy strong point. The latter was taken by surprise, falling within 10 minutes, "The Keep" proved to be somewhat harder. For several hours the battle was fought, the victory coming as a result of determined parties of bombers. At 4.45 the Hun tried in vain to retake "The Keep". The 55th Division are believed to be the only engaged Division to hold its line intact in the Spring of 1918. The next two days passed without incident, and the weary remnants of the Liverpool Scottish were relieved on the night of 15/16th April. The weeks fighting had cost the battalion 3 Officers killed and 63 other ranks killed or died of wounds, a further 8 Officers and 127 other ranks wounded.

Amongst the mortally wounded was Private Lloydd who was casualty evacuated to Etaples the site of a vast military reinforcement camp. The area also contained numerous military hospitals through which the wounded passed before returning to Blighty. As a result of wounds received during the Battle of Givenchy, Private Lloydd died. He is interred within Plot XXIX, Row D, Grave 1A at the large Etaples Military Cemetery, Pas de Calais, France. Etaples is a town 27 kilometres south of Boulogne, the military cemetery is 2 kms to the north of the town, on the west side of the road to Boulogne. The cemetery is the final resting place of 11,000 men including 657 Germans, a permanent reminder of the vast military complex which was formerly based there.

JOSEPH SUTTON

SERGEANT   24472   11(SERVICE) CHESHIRES

Joseph Sutton was the son of John James and Elizabeth Sutton who were the tenant Farmers of Reeds Farm, Leasowe. Although the farm no longer exists, that farm track gave its name to the Reeds Lane as we know today. Joseph was a farmer by profession and was probably employed on his parents' farm. When Joseph married Martha the couple resided at 13 Neville Road, Wallasey.

In late December 1914 Joseph and his Moreton pals paid their weekly visit to the Argyle Theatre and on this particular evening a Major Murray appealed to the audience for Army volunteers. During this rousing recruiting speech Joseph Sutton leapt up and volunteered, simultaneously offering the services of his Moreton pals. This led to a recruitment meeting at Moreton where thirteen men took the Kings shilling, the men served with the 11/ Cheshires. As he was over thirty years of age, Joseph Sutton must have been one of the senior men in the battalion.

In the Spring of 1918 the 11/Cheshires including Sergeant Sutton were still serving on the Western Front, where the battalion had weathered the storm of Operation Michael. The exhausted German infantry faced increasing resistance, on 5th April the sixteen day old offensive was called off, the anticipated knock out blow had failed. Due to excesive casualties a modified German attack on a smaller scale was then launched in Flanders.

The 19th and 25th Divisions contained the 9th, 10th and 11th Cheshires. The men of these battalions were worn out after the strenuous fighting on the Somme in March. The Divisions were relocated to the Messines Front where a much quieter existence offered an opportunity to recuperate. This was familiar territory to Sergeant Sutton for the 11/Cheshires had come full circle, the original draught had first entered the line at Ploegsteert Wood three years earlier. On 10th April 1918 the 11/Cheshires where in the line at Deulemont near Ploegsteert, Belguim. At 6am a German attack which outnumbered the defenders by at least 5 to 1, unexpectedly appeared out of the thick morning fog, swiftly over-running the front and support posts. The 11/Cheshires then fell back to a position West of Ploegsteert, the troops either side of the 11th then fell back. Although this left the battalion in a precarious position they held their line until ordered to occupy a line straddling the Romarin to Ploegsteert Road near Regina Farm. The enemy had entered Ploegsteert Wood and were advancing towards the village of Ploegsteert, when at about 5.30pm the 11/Cheshires launched a counter attack against Ploegsteert. Amongst the battalions 17 other ranks who were killed in action on this day was Sergeant Joseph Sutton.

The 35 year old soldier was killed on 10th April 1918, his grave if any is not known. His sacrifice is recorded on the Ploegsteert Memorial to the missing which stands 12.5K south of Ieper. Within the impressive memorial panels contain the names of 11,447 missing men, the Cheshire Regiment casualties being located on panels 4 and 5.

Despite the defenders' valiant efforts the Hun gradually tightened his grip on Flanders, with an eye as ever for Ypres. In rapid succession Messines village and a portion of the Messines-Wytschaete ridge was lost and Armentieres was hastily evacuated by the British. On 11th April, Field Marshall Haig issued a special order of the day, part of which included the famous stirring command "There is no other course open to us but to fight it out. Every position must be held to the last man - there must be no retirement. With our backs to the wall and believing in the justice of our cause each one of us must fight to the end". Allied reinforcements of two British and one Australian division now arrived in Flanders in an increasingly desperate attempt to stem the advancing wave of field grey clad infantrymen, whose attacks were now appearing to waiver.

Meanwhile at home on the Wirral the local German prisoners-of-war were now working on repairs to the sea wall embankment at Leasowe, when they prevented a possibly tragic accident. A boat containing several local youths capsized while some distance from the shore, and several prisoners plunged into the sea and rescued them.

OSWALD W HARDCASTLE

SERGEANT   24031   10(SERVICE) CHESHIRES

Oswald Hardcastle was one of three brothers, namely Ernest and Thomas, who all resided at Moreton. The three brothers served with separate battalions of the Cheshire Regiment. Upon the outbreak of hostilities Oswald attested to the newly formed 13th battalion of Cheshires. He was one of the original battalion members, possibly a self-assured man who instantly received promotion to Corporal of 3 Company.

This local raised battalion took part in the infamous Battle of the Somme. As the cream of Kitchener's New Army slowly advanced across No Mans Land, they were mown down in their thousands by the German machine gunners. In September 1916, Oswald and his brother Thomas were in hospital, recovering from wounds. The wounds most likely had been sustained during the Somme attack. When fully recovered Sergeant Hardcastle returned to the blood soaked battle fields of France and Belgium.

By 1918 the carnage had killed and maimed so many men that all the front line infantry battalions were seriously under strength. This resulted in the merging of numerous battalions, and despite the protestations of the local members of Parliament, the Wirral battalion lost its local identity when it was disbanded on 16th February 1918. The majority of the 13th battalion, including Sergeant Hardcastle were merged with the 10(Service) Cheshire battalion. From the 9th to the 11th April the Battalion formed part of the hard pressed force engaged in the Battle of Estaires.

By the 11th April the German attack had gained their objectives of the top of the Messines Ridge and also Hill 63. This resulted in an order for the troops to fall back to a new line. At 5.45am the enemy broke through the 75th Brigade front rapildy creating a two mile gap. Once again with their flanks exposed the defending British fell back and reformed their defences. On the evening of 10th April the 10/Cheshires were in a sharp salient along the north edge of Ploegsteert Wood, holding a 2,000 yard front. Shortly after midday the next day 7th Brigade Headquarters ordered the withdrawal of the 1/Wiltshires and 10/Cheshires who were now in the catacombs at the base of Hill 63. This order was misconstrued, the battalions on the Hill believing they were to hold to the last man. When the enemy attacked, one company of the 10/Cheshires launched a valiant but unsuccessful counter attack. Although totally surrounded a few of the encircled defenders managed to fight their way back to the British lines west of Neuve Eglise.

Sergeant Hardcastle was killed in action in one of the above actions, the 31 year old Moreton soldier has no known grave, his death is recorded on the Ploegsteert Memorial, Belgium. Miss M Harding, who was Oswald's next-of-kin, received the tragic news that her brother had been killed on 11th April 1918. The Moreton War Memorial incorrectly records Sergeant Hardcastle's death occurred whilst serving with the disbanded 13th Cheshires. From the three gallant Hardcastle brothers only Tom Hardcastle survived the Great War.

JOSEPH EVANS

**PRIVATE   15982   2/SOUTH LANCASHIRE
REGIMENT**

Joe Evans was a Moreton lad born and bred. He was the eldest son of Thomas W and Catherine Evans, who resided at 13 Smithy Lane (now Netherton Road), Moreton. Thomas Evans was an old employee of Mersey Railway, who also had two other sons serving with the colours.

In early November 1914, Joe Evans travelled to Liverpool and volunteered. The patriotic youth proudly enlisted into the 2/ South Lancashire Regiment, the Prince of Wales Volunteers. This particular infantry battalion was part of the original BEF which had suffered massive casualties. The battlion reinforcements were volunteers who receieved the bare rudiments of military training before being hastly despatched to reinforce the Western Front. Amongst their ranks was Joe Evans who entered the front line trenches of France in early May 1915.

Shortly after arriving at the front he forwarded a letter to his sister, (wife of the posted as missing Pte W Massey). Private Evans stated he was alright and referred to two letters he had received from Sid Massey and Fred McGuire and a number of parcels received from his many Moreton friends, particularly those from Ted. His letter continued and describes a miraculous escape,

I have lost my mate he was hit in the arm a week ago by a grenade. Five of them got wounded by the same grenade. I who happened to be in the middle of the lot

113

didn't get a scratch. It was hell with the lid off up to that place, only don't say anything to mother. We are having things a bit easier now.

The letter probably relates to the Battle of Bapaume, during which half the battalion were casualties.

For almost three years Private Evans survived amongst the churned and blasted earthworks of France and Flanders. At the beginning of April 1918, the 25th Division, which the 2/ South Lancs constituted a part of, took over the quiet Ploegsteert sector. The next morning the Germans launched a series of attacks on a 7,000 yard front bounded by the River Lys and Douve. The attacking Germans gradually gained more ground, as the Allies fell back and regrouped. On the 10th the battalion received orders to occupy a position on the high ground 2,000 yards west of Ploegsteert. Later that day two companies assisted the Cheshires in the doomed counter attack on Ploegsteert village. Under cover of darkness the battalion relocated to a new line in front of Romarin, covering Neuve Eglise the new position being unsuccessfully attacked twice that day. The following day (April 12th) at dawn the battalion's position was heavily shelled, part of the battalion relocated to form a defensive flank along the Romarin to Neuve Eglise. At 2pm the remainder of the battalion were again attacked in force and despite strong resistance were driven back to a position 500 yards south east of Neuve Eglise, where they dug in. The following morning at 5am, the Germans attacked under cover of a thick mist, the defensive flank crumbled, a strategic withdrawal was then made to a line held by the 8th Highland Light Infantry, on high ground south west of Neuve Eglise. The advancing German infantry again attacked, the attack was repulsed with the Germans suffering heavy casualties. The 2/South Lancs, and the Highlanders advanced 800 yards and took up new positions. By 6am the position become untenable and they were forced to withdraw to the Ravelsberg a strategic hill east of Bailleul.

Numbered amongst the dead and dying of these ferocious attacks was young Joseph Evans. A twenty four old soldier who died on 13th April. The fortunes of war denied the Moreton soldier a known final resting place. He is however commemorated on the Ploegsteert Memorial to the missing which stands in Berks Cemetery Extension. This is located 12.5km south of Ieper (Ypres) town centre, on the N365 leading from Ieper to Mesen (Messines).

GEORGE EDWIN ENNION

PRIVATE 39981 8(SERVICE) SOUTH LANCASHIRES

George Ennion was born in Waverton near Chester, his parents were farm workers. The family later moved to the Moreton area where there was plenty of employment for those working on the land. It is thought that George was employed as a farm hand, a traditional Ennion occupation which is still practised by the family to this day. In April 1914, the church of Christ Church was the scene of the marriage of George and Anne Stanley Pownall, who was described as a spinster of Hoylake.

George and Anne resided in the village at Chapel Lane (now Barnston Lane). Married life was soon to be interrupted by military service. George Ennion travelled to Birkenhead where he enlisted into the Prince of Wales Volunteers, the South Lancashire Regiment. Private Ennion served with the 8th (Service) battalion which was raised at Warrington in September 1914, as a direct response to the call to arms for a volunteer army. The new army eventually consisted of over 500 battalions and was known at the time as Kitchener's Army. The battalion was attached to the 75th Brigade, 25th Division which contained several North West battalions. In November 1914 the 8/South Lancashires were based at Codford, and later underwent training at army camps at Bournemouth, Wokingham and finally Aldershot. The long awaited opportuntiy to have a crack at the Kaiser finally arrived, when the battalion sailed for France in September 1915. George Ennion served with the 8th Battalion until they were disbanded on 16th February 1918, he was then transferred to the 2nd Battalion. He would therefore have been engaged in the same battles as his fellow Moretonian the late Private Joe Evans.

The Battle of Lys continued unabated and by mid April Germany had captured the Ravelsberg, Mont de Lille and Crucifix Corner; these victories were gained despite tenacious resistance. From 10th to 16 April the 2/S Lancs casualties amounted to 16 Officers killed and 646 other ranks killed, wounded or missing which indicates the severity of the fighting. A fortnight previously the Battalion had lost almost fifty per cent of its strength, its fighting force being made up to strength by the arrival of young soldiers who fought magnificently. Once again the Battalion was a skeleton, two companies were combined with survivors of the 75th Brigade into a composite battalion, named the 75th

Battalion. The unit was employed under the 34th Division as a mobile reserve without, however, going into action. The unit was based in the Monts de Cats area, and only existed for two hellish days, the 19th and 20th April. The 34th Division were constantly threatened and this resulted in constant counter marching by the 75th Battalion into areas bombarded by continuous shell fire. There was no respite of a night as the bivouacs and transport lines were bombed from the air, consequently nobody had any rest.

The battalion resumed its original identity on 21st April when they were again made up to strength. after four days rest near Poperinghe, they were placed in reserve for the partially successful attack on Kemmel. The role of the battlion was to counter attack if necessary, and also to form a defensive flank should the enemy capture the Scherpenberg.

It is assumed that Private George Edwin Ennion was mortally wounded while serving with the 75th Battalion, he was a casualty and was then evacuated to Boulogne. The twenty six year old soldier died there on 28 April 1918, and his mortal remains are interred in the Boulogne Eastern Cemetery, grave reference IX A 49. The cemetery which is one of the largest in the area stands on the high ground on the eastern side of Boulogne on the road to St Omer. Boulogne was one of the main landing and medical centres for the BEF. Nearly 12,000 British soldiers are buried in and around the town.

JOHN WILLIAM FRENCH

PRIVATE   56378   14(SERVICE) ROYAL WELSH FUSILIERS

John William French was born in Edmonton, Greater London. The infant was christened with exactly the same names as his father. At an unknown date John W French junior settled in Moreton. He married Elizabeth Jane Peers and the couple had five children. The family resided at 10 Stamford (now Willaston) Road. Before joining the military he travelled to London, this could possibly have been to advise his father of his decision to join the colours, after which he visited the local recruitment centre at Stratford and attested, to King and Country. He originally served as a Private number 25874 with the Cheshire Regiment. At a later date he was transferred to the Llandudno raised 14th Service battalion of the Royal Welsh Fusiliers (RWF). The battalion served in France from December 1915.

The beginning of April 1918 heralded a welcome respite for the 113th Infantry Brigade, of which the RWF formed a part. The Division was preoccupied in preparations for the defence of the town of Albert. The War Diary of the 14th RWF Battalion records that the Spring days were spent in field exercises. The ribald comments of the battle weary soldiers who were ordered to practice advancing in artillery formation, repelling enemy counter attacks, etc is not recorded. On the 11th April the battalion marched to the Somme villages of Contay and Vadencourt where they entered the trench system. The battalion spent several days toiling in working and wiring parties. They entered the front line trenches on the 16th. During the following 48 hours small reconnoitring patrols were constantly despatched into No Mans Land. After this hazardous period the fusiliers were relieved, but unfortunately there was to be no respite. While A and B companies returned to the night working parties, C and D companies spent the morning practising for tomorrow's assault. The over-worked men were granted an afternoon's rest, on the eve of battle.

On 22nd April, Zero hour was at 7.30pm, as the whistles blew the 113th Brigade advanced across the battle field. As C and D companies of the 14/RWF advanced, B company moved up and occupied their vacated position. While our artillery cover proved to be haphazard the enemy very quickly laid a barrage near our front line. Well sited enemy machine guns swept the advancing lines, resulting in heavy casualties. Neither company reached their first objective, managing to gain only 150 yards of territory.

The battalion sustained the following casualties 3 Officers killed, 2 wounded, the other ranks losses were 6 killed, 95 wounded and 14 missing. Private French would have been included amongst the missing. As a result the 35 year old soldier has no known grave. The town of Albert fell to the Germans four days later.

Approximately 6 kilometres north east of Albert lies the village of Pozieres. On the outskirts of the village lies Pozieres British Cemetery, which is situated on the north side of the extremely busy D929 road. In 1916 the cemetery started as a simple battle field grave yard. The Germans buried 57 of their dead here in 1918, but these graves were removed after the war. The cemetery contains mostly Australian graves. The cemetery is bounded by stone rubble walls. Affixed to three of the walls are stone tablets bearing the names of the missing dead grouped under their Regiments. Panels 36 and 37 of the Pozieres Memorial are dedicated to the Royal Welsh Fusiliers. The name of Private John William French is carved with pride on the memorial.

John William French and Family

Photograph courtesy of Mrs. E. Conway.

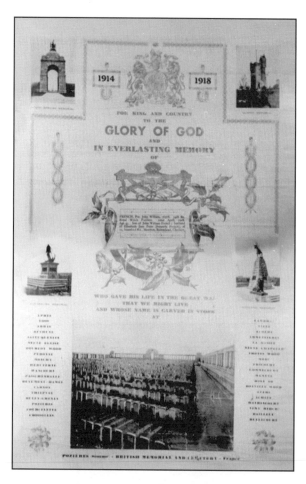

In the 1920s framed commemorative scrolls such as the above were given pride of place in the family homes of the fallen. Commercially produced, the bereaved families simply inserted the deceased's detail in the centre panel. This cherished keepsake is shown courtesy of the Conway family.

ANDREW BOWMAN
PRIVATE   94195   17/(SERVICE) KINGS LIVERPOOL

Andrew Bowman was a true native of Moreton. He is thought to be the son of Annie Bowman who resided at St Elmo, Reeds Lane. The house still stands alongside the River Birkett. During the war he attended the recruiting office at Hoylake Town Hall. He attested to the Cheshire Regiment, later serving as a Private with the regimental number of 44223. Initially he served with the 3(Reserve) Cheshires who were based at Bidston Hill, as part of the Mersey Defences, while fulfilling a secondary role as a training battlion. Some time later Private Bowman transferred to the 17th Battlion of the Kings Liverpool Regiment, which is perhaps better known as the 1st City Battalion of the illustrious Liverpool Pals. While on home leave Private Bowman married Mary Jane Goldsmith, a widow of Wallasey. The ceremony was held at Christ Church in early June 1915. After almost a year's training the 17th Battalion disembarked at Boulogne on 7th November 1915.

As part of the 89th Brigade, the Liverpool Pals served with honour on the Western Front. The Liverpool Pals were amongst the most successful troops who fought on 1st July, successfully capturing their objectives, with minimal casualties. The final year of the war witnessed three Liverpool Pals battalions moving into the front line trenches near Voormezeele, Flanders (Belgium). On the night of 27th April 1918 the 17/Kings found themselves preparing to defend the line between Convent Lane and the Voormezeele defences. Protecting their right front from the advancing Germans were their fellow Kingsmen. The Battle of Lys,more accurately known by the French as the third battle of Flanders, commenced on 9th April 1918 producing a series of previously mentioned set battles.

On the 29th April the penultimate day of the campaign, fighting occurred near Voormezeele. This developed into a particularly fierce assault, now known as the Battle of Scherpenberg. At 1pm the Hun breached the defences to the left of the 17th Pals, forcing back the front line. The Pals reorganised and managed to hold the position, although later on the enemy again broke through almost encircling two Pals, companies. Despite fierce resistance "A" Company were totally surrounded and the embattled survivors were taken prisoner. The deperate struggle raged for five hours, and in an attempt to alleviate the situation the Commanding Officer committed his reserve company to a counter attack to be launched at 7.45pm. Approximately ten minutes prior to the counter attack the Germans laid a fierce artillery bombardment all along the front. The counter attack was cancelled due to a three hour storm of steel and explosive, which rained down on the defenders. Following the bombardment the Pals formed a defensive flank, successfully repulsing a series of attacks. After successfully holding the line the 89th Brigade were relieved at the conclusion of the Battle of Lys on the 1 May 1918.

The events of 29th April 1918 claimed the lives of 64 Liverpool Pals, one of whom was Private Andrew Bowman. The 31 year old soldier has no known grave, but his sacrifice is recorded at Tyne Cot Memorial Cemetery, Belgium, which is the largest British military cemetery in the world. As the massive Menin Gate memorial to the missing could not contain the names of all the men who disappeared in Belgium, one of the cemetery's boundaries is in effect a vast wall etched with the names of those without a known grave. The missing members of the Liverpool Regiment are commemorated on panels 31 to 34.

The village memorials state Private Bowman was killed while serving with the 3/Cheshires, this has proven incorrect.

The great retreat of 1918 produced scores of distingushed defences and assaults which are too numerous to contain within these pages. As there appears to be no documented account of any "Moreton Patriots" involvement in this critical period the following paragraph gives only a skeletal account of this crucial period during which the ultimate outcome of the war was virtually determined. Thwarted by increasing resistance Lundendorff launched his troops against the Bailleau - Ypres front but they made only marginal headway. The Georgette offensive was now called off, against all the odds the bloodied yet unbowed Allies had retained the key towns of Amiens, Ypres and the vital Channel ports. The advance which had cost Germany over 348,000 casualties also gravely weakened the combined Allied strength. Ludendorff was well aware that French Reserves had reinforced the British sector so he now prepared to attack the quiet French sector, which also contained five divisions of resting British troops. On 27th May the Hun advanced sweeping all before them initially advancing up to 12 miles a day. A week later they crossed the River Marne and were now only approximately fifty miles from Paris. The advance on their capital was halted by the French who significantly fought alongside the United States 2nd and 3rd Divisions. Undeterred the Germans successfully attacked elsewhere, and on 11th June the French counter-attacked, the infantry being supported by tanks and low flying aircraft. Consequently another Teutonic gamble ground to a halt. On 4th July a small scale yet meticulous Australian and American assault on Hamel captured its objective in ninety minutes making the future look grim for Germany. In mid-July the increasingly desperate Ludendorff, who was still convinced the BEF could be beaten in Flanders, attacked either side of Reims. A massive counterstroke burst upon the invaders between the Aisne and Marne and by August 6th the Germans had lost 168,000 men, of which 29,000 were prisoners, and also 800 artillery pieces had been captured. The tide had finally turned and the path was now paved for an Allied victory.

HENRY WILSON

PRIVATE   201358   1/4 CHESHIRES

Henry Wilson was better known as Harry. A Moreton man born and bred, he was one of the sons of Mary and Henry Wilson. The family resided at Felicity Cottage, Moreton, and decades later the dwelling was demolished and Felicity Grove was built on the cleared site.

Harry Wilson is the soldier second from the right
Photograph provided courtesy of the Mitchell Family.

During the Great War, Harry Wilson served as a Private with the local Territorial Battalion, the 1/4 Cheshires who were based at Grange Road West. The battalion saw approximately four months action at Gallipoli, and following the withdrawal from the deadly Peninsula the battalion went to Egypt. As an envisaged attack by the Turks on the Suez Canal never transpired, the troops were relocated to Palestine where they were again engaged against the Turks. In the later stages of the war, a severe shortage of manpower on the European battlefields resulted in the redeployment of troops from all over the globe. The 1/7 and 1/4 Cheshires were amongst the forces despatched to France to bolster the under strength Divisions, arriving on 29th June 1918. Two days later they joined the 102nd Brigade, 34th Divison at Proven. Despite the fact that the Cheshires had been away from their families for over 18 months, only a minority of their number were granted leave. Despite their arduous journey, the war weary troops were plunged into battle immediately in the hell on earth, best known as the Western Front.

The battle orders on July 23rd required the storming of the ridge, which overlooked the unspoilt countryside between the rivers Aisne and Ourcq. This area was unlike the trench strewn landscape so typical of the old front lines, but virginal countryside to the rear of the old German front line. Little was known about the future battlefield area or the strength of the foe who lay in concealment in the surrounding forests. Two battalions of Cheshires were involved in the attack, the 7/Cheshires objective being the capture of Reogny Wood, and after this was gained the 4/Cheshires were to press on and take Hartennes. The battle zone was swathed in standing corn which caused problems for the slowly advancing 7/Cheshires who resorted to firing Lewis Guns from the hip. After gaining 1200 yards under heavy machine gun fire, the Territorials halted and waited for the French infantry who had failed to capture Tigny. The 1/4 Battalion dug in alongside the 1/7 Cheshires. By now both Cheshire battalions were pinned down by heavy machine gun and artillery fire. The Hun then laid down a barrage of gas shells, and the men of the 1/4 being inexperienced in gas warfare were slow to react. On this day the 1/4 Battalion lost 4 Officers and 276 other ranks, the 1/7 Cheshires suffered 180 deaths. During the night the survivors of both battalions regrouped alongside the French. Unfortunately worse was to come as the following day both Cheshire Battalions were heavily shelled by our own artillery.

A mortally wounded Private Henry Wilson was evacuated to the vast hospital complex on the outskirts of the Cathedral town of

Rouen, where he died of wounds on 31st July 1918. All the evidence intimated the 25 year old Moreton soldier died a slow horrendous death through gas poisoning, attributed to events on 23rd July. Mrs Beecroft, a relation of Private Wilson, confirmed her ancestor died as a result of gas warfare.

Private Wilson is interred at St Sever Cemetery Extension, Rouen, Seine-Maritime, France, his grave reference is Plot Q, Row 4, Grave H1. The cemetery commemorates over 8,500 World War One and 300 Second World War casualties. St Sever Cemetery and Extension lies approximately 3 kilometres south of Rouen Cathedral and a short distance west of the road from Rouen to Elbeuf.

The brother of the late Harry Wilson was also a combatant, and several weeks after his brother's demise Private Joe Wilson was wounded. In late August Mrs Wilson of 20 Stamford (Willaston) Road received news that her husband had been wounded in the head and leg, and was now recovering in an English hospital. The former employee of Moreton Brick Works joined the Loyal North Lancashire Regiment soon after the outbreak of war, and up to now had served in France for two years. The Moreton soldier survived the war.

Joe Wilson

Joe Wilson on right in civilian clothes.
Both photographs courtesy of the Mitchell family.

ADRIAN PERCY LATHAM

CORPORAL 356826 1/10(SCOTTISH) KINGS

Adrian P Latham was born in Liverpool in 1891, his parents were Agnes and Maurice Latham. The young man is known to have resided at "The Cot", West Baldwin, Isle of Man prior to residing at "Dandyrigg", Chapel Lane. The building was long ago converted for retail purposes, remaining as the first shop in Barnston Lane, Moreton.

On the 3rd November 1915 Adrian Latham travelled to Liverpool, where he attested to the 10th Territorial Battalion of the Kings Liverpool Regiment. The Liverpool Scottish were formed in Liverpool on 27th January 1900 for service in the Boer War. The new recruit was issued with the Regimental number 5502, his army number was 356826. The Private soldier was posted to B Company of the 3/10 Battalion, serving initially at the canvas Army camp in Weeton, which is approximately three miles from Blackpool. With the onset of Winter the tents proved inadequate, prompting a move to better billets situated at the North Shore, Blackpool. The promenade was utilised for military training. Private Latham and his comrades formed the 14th Draft of the Kilt wearing Liverpool Scottish battalion which departed for France and Flanders on 19 May 1916.

Upon arrival the battalion was utilised as casualty replacements for the 9/Liverpools. On the 27th August 1916 Private Latham joined the 1/10 battalion, where he was posted to 9 Platoon, Y Company. On 13th September 1916 the Liverpool Scottish were in the locality of Longueval near Delville Wood, where Private Latham was severely wounded. As a result the soldier was invalided back to Blighty on 27th October 1916, resulting in a lengthy period of hospitalisation. While convalescing the wounded veteran served in the United Kingdom, possibly assisting in training recruits. During this period the Moreton soldier was promoted to the rank of Corporal.

Returning to the ravaged battle fields of France and Flanders, he endured a further two years of horror. The curtain was gradually coming down on the war and on 8th August near Amiens the Allies counter-attacked at dawn and by noon had captured all their objectives. Lundendorff wrote "August 8th was the black day of the German army in the history of this war". Remorseless Allied attacks from all directions were steadily pushing back the increasingly demoralised Germans, some units surrendering with only token resistance. Near the end of August 1918 the enemy in the vicinity of the 1/10 Kings began to retire from their front line trenches. Following a 12 day tour of duty in the trenches the Liverpool Scottish spent a 6 day rest period at the hutments at Vaudricourt Camp. The battalion returned to the line on 8th September 1918, when they occupied the vacated old German front line. The sector proved to be particularly hostile as the enemy artillery bombarded their old position for 10 days. A further hazard consisted of explosive booby traps left behind by former occupants of the trench system. On the 20th September 1918 the 1/5 South Lancashires captured Spook Trench and the Pumping Stations in conjunction with the 19th Division who reached the main La Bassee Road.

An inherent danger of occupying a former enemy trench was that the enemy artillery was all too familiar with the trench's exact map reference and defensive capabilities. While the Liverpool Scottish were located near the main La Bassee Road, Coporal Latham was made aware of imminent danger, as he attempted to warn his comrades he was killed by shellfire. The 27 year old warrior was killed in action on 21/9/18, which is approximately six weeks prior to the cessation of hostilities.

The mortal remains of Corporal Latham are interred at Grave Reference III E 27, Houchin British Cemetery, which is situated near Bethune, within the province of Pas de Calais, France. The incumbents of the war graves cemetery are mainly casualties from the 55th (West Lancashire) Division, who died during the Battle of Lys. The Moreton Patriot is also commemorated on a Manx memorial.

Corporal A P Latham

During 1918 few Moreton events were deemed of interest to the readership of the Wirral newspapers. The papers were constrained by increased censorship, and a disillusioned readership so often misled in the past by jingoistic reporting of military disasters, appear to have preferred to read about more mundane matters. At a time when the Hun was in retreat at the beginning of August, questions were asked in the House of Commons concerning the departure of German prisoners from Leasowe Castle. The army camp at Bidston had been hastily built at the beginning of the war, the barracks consisted of an assortment of wooden huts, which were now in a state of disrepair. The army enviously eyed the superior accommodation of the Hun prisoners at Leasowe Castle, and proposed an exchange of billets. Although the residents of the sleepy village of Bidston vigorously opposed the move, their protestations were to no avail.

The bungalow town at Moreton fore shore was also causing concern. In late September the Borough Surveyor expressed grave concerns regarding their sanitation. Unlike the established village the campers endured squalid conditions. At one location 619 adults and 424 children occupied an assortment of tents, vans and bungalows. While on Shore Fields 196 tents, vans and bungalows provided shelter for 314 adults and 257 children. Despite all this the campers were contented with their lot and stoutly defended their life style. The sites were gradually improved, and the tents gave way to bungalows which remained in use until the intrjduction of council houses decades later.

Leasowe Castle, one of Wirral's most historical hotels

At the end of 1917 volunteers from the Mesopotania Expeditionary force made up "Dunsterforce" and amongst their number was Sergeant Biddle. The hand-picked force less than a battalion strong was led by Major General Dunsterville (the hero of Rudyard Kipling's "Stalky and Co") and served in Western Persia.

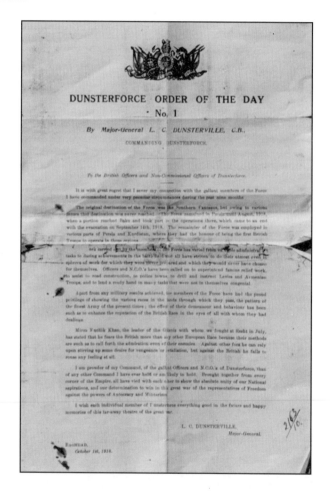

Document courtesy of Mr F Biddle.

At the beginning of this narrative an emphasis was placed on the raising of the 11th Battalion of the Cheshire Regiment, which appeared to be the favoured battalion of the Moreton volunteers. It is therefore appropriate to record the demise of the battalion, which was another victim of battalion mergers. On average one in every four battalions was disbanded due to manpower shortages. On 17th June 1918 the 11th Cheshires were reduced to a Cadre, which is basically the nucleus of a battalion. This small force was merged with the 1/6 Cheshires who absorbed 16 Officers and 492 men of the Kitchener raised 11th battalion. The battlion was officially disbanded in France on 3rd August 1918.

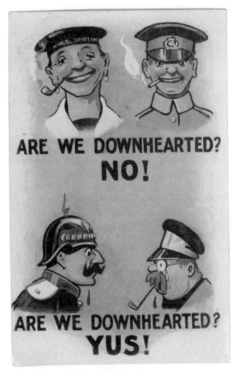

The British propaganda machine used every opportunity to drive the message home. The nation's mania for postcards proved an ideal means for stimulating National morale, the Hun being frequently depicted as an overweight, poor sighted buffoon.

ERIC MUTCH

COMPANY SERGEANT MAJOR 16340 9 (SERVICE) CHESHIRE REGIMENT

Eric Mutch was the son of Mr and Mrs Thomas Mutch, who resided at Smithy Lane, Moreton. Young Eric was an employee of Thomas's the Moreton Grocers. Immediately after the declaration of war, Eric joined the Cheshire Regiment. He is recorded as being one of the youngest men from the Moreton district to volunteer, his age at enlistment is believed to have been 17 years. The 9th Battalion was formed at Chester on 13 September 1914 in response to Kitchener's appeal for volunteers and these men were part of the first 200,000 to volunteer. After completion of training on Salisbury Plain the battalion departed for France, arriving at Boulogne on 16th July 1915. The 9th Cheshires first tasted action in the Battle of Loos, which commenced on 25th September 1915. The Kitchener volunteers served with distinction along the length and breadth of the Western Front, for the duration of the Great War.

In February 1916 the Moreton soldier was promoted to the rank of Sergeant, which was quite an achievement for a 19 years old man. An even more extraordinary feat was, in rapidly attaining a further promotion to the rank of Company Sergeant Major (CSM). During his military service in France the young volunteer was twice wounded. His bravery in the field was recognised by the award of the Distinguished Conduct Medal, there were only 194 of these medals awarded to the Regiment throughout the Great War. Sergeant Mutch was decorated by the Field Marshall Commander for meritorious services on the Somme. The citation reads:

By his splendid example and complete disregard of danger, he gave invaluable help to his Officer, and kept his men well together at a most trying and critical time. When his company was withdrawing he remained until the last, and issued orders for the covering fire. All this time he was working under heavy enemy fire.

In September 1918 the London Gazette recorded CSM Mutch, as having been awarded the Italian Bronze medal for military valour on the Italian Front. This award is attributed to the period of December 1917 while CSM Mutch was probably serving with the 1/Cheshires, the only Cheshire battalion with the Battle Honour of Italy.

Company Sergeant Major Mutch DCM survived the war.

Photograph provided courtesy of M Waters.

Three Moreton soldiers pose for a snapshot outside of a once typical Moreton Cottage. They are from left to right, F Potter, E Mutch and O Hardcastle. Visible on the lower left sleeve of CSM Mutch is a two inch (5cm) vertical wound stripe. None of the soldiers are wearing their tunic belts. The sandstone cottage was known as Jeffreys or Wilsons cottage, the confusion arising as Miss Wilson married John Jeffrey. The now demolished cottage stood approximately facing the future site of Sacred Heart Church.

FREDRICK SUMNER CLARK

LIEUTENANT   10(SCOTTISH) KINGS LIVERPOOL

On 1st February 1885 Fredrick Sumner Clark was born in Birkenhead, the second son of Mr and Mrs Fred Clark. His father was employed as a Foreman in the wood working department of Cammell Lairds Shipbuilders, for almost 50 years. The young boy was educated at the Claughton Higher Grade School and Liverpool University. Upon completing his education, he served his apprenticeship with Messrs George Wall and Co, provision merchants. In 1900 he joined the company, rising to the position of Departmental Manager. Fred Clark was specially noted for his social and religious work in Claughton and Oxton districts, especially on behalf of the young people of St Michael's Church in Carlton Road. In 1911 he married Miss Florence Bolton, and the newly weds resided at 14 Loretto Road, Wallasey. Another known address was 12 Rugby Road, Wallasey. Fred Clark then became the Sunday school, teacher and Superintendant of children's services at St Lukes Church, Poulton. after 17 years service with Wall and Co, Fred Clark departed in April 1917 to join the Army.

Mr Clark enlisted into the ranks of the 10(Scottish) battalion of the Kings Liverpool Regiment, attesting on 5th April 1917. His first posting was to the 3/10 Reserve battalion which was based at Park Hall Camp, Oswestry. After six months in the ranks he was selected for a commission, and trained in the Officer Training Corps at Tweezledown. He was Gazetted as a 2/Lieutenant on 19th December 1917, serving with the 10th KLR. After reporting for duty on 22nd January 1918 he rejoined the 3/10 battalion at Oswestry. The battalion was a Reserve battalion and did not serve overseas. 2/Lt Clark then served in France and Flanders, where he was originally posted to the 2/10 Kings battalion, before being attached to the 1/4 Seaforth Highlanders. This was the Ross Highland territorial battalion which was attached to the 51st (Highland) Division.

During July 1918 the Allies held the German advances and it was during this critical period that the bravery of Lt Clark was officially recognised. His bravery in the field resulted in the awarding of the French gallantry award the Croix de Guerre. Fate decreed he would never personally receive the award as it was not Gazetted until 10th October 1919.

Less than a month before the end of the war, Lieutenant Clark was acting as an Intelligence Officer at a location near the French village of Lieu St Amand, near Cambrai. On 14th October 1918 he was killed by a shell burst, which also wounded his Commanding Officer and also the Adjutant of the battalion. A brother Officer wrote the following to the fallen Officer's widow:

As our intelligence officer your Husband did great and noble work. His untiring energy was the wonder of all. We loved him for that, but we loved him more for his heroism in the face of danger, for his nobility of soul and for his true comradeship at all times. He died as he lived, a great brave Christian gentlemen.

While another Officer provided the following observation:

War to him was a thing quite out of keeping with his kindly nature, yet during the whole time he was with us no-one in the battalion did better work.

The 33 year old Officer left behind a Widow with a recently born son. Lieutenant Clark was originally interred within the British Cemetery of Thun St Martin, approximately four miles east of Cambrai. Enquiries with the Commonwealth War Graves Commission revealed the cemetery was abandoned shortly after the war, due to maintenance or access problems. The remains of the soldiers were re-interred at the nearby Naves Communal Cemetery Extension, which is 4 miles away from Cambrai, or more accurately a half mile south west of Naves Halte, on the Cambrai Road. Most of the burials are a result of the October 1918 second battle of Cambrai, one of the last battles of the Hindenburg Line. The town was used as a German garrison base until 8th October, and as the Bosche retreated they mined and fired the town. After the war the shattered remains of the Cambrai were adopted by the County Borough of Birkenhead, ironically the birth place of Fred Clark.

As a token of their esteem towards their former Sunday school teacher the parishioners of St Lukes Church, Poulton placed a dedicated brass plaque within the church. The late Officer is also commemorated on the Roll of Honour for the Parish of Poulton. He is also featured within the pages of Liverpool's Scroll of Fame, from which his portrait has been reproduced.

By mid October the Belgian army had entered Ostend, the French had entered the city of Laon and British and Empire troops were holding a line along the Lys. In most sectors the retiring Hun fought fierce reargaurd actions displaying all their customary Teutonic defiance. The object of Lundendorff's strategic withdrawal was to retire to the German border where an armistice could be negotiated from a position of strength. If the negotiations were protracted the time gained would enable the re-organisation of German forces. Throughout the withdrawal the Allied advance was hampered by blown bridges and a series of rivers and watercourses which caused severe problems in the advancement of tanks and artillery while the infantry men crossed rivers by any improvised means. During these respites the Germans wired and excavated the terrain ahead of the Allied advance and gave no quarter in their flight to the outreaches of the great forest of Mormal, an ideal location for a prolonged defensive action. The Allied forces anticpated such a manoeuvre and aimed to isolate the retreating army from the Fatherland, and on 23rd October Haig unleased 150,000 troops across a fifteen mile front. The advance to victory necessitated numerous attacks and counter attacks, one such engagement claiming the life of the final Moreton Warrior to die on a foreign battlefield.

W A HERBERT MERCER

PRIVATE   41156   1/SOUTH WALES BORDERERS

William Arthur Herbert Mercer was born in Liverpool circa 1898, he was named after his father William. During the war years the Mercers resided at "Riverside", The Common, Moreton which may have been one of the shanty town bungalows.

Herbert Mercer took the Kings shilling at Liverpool and originally served with the Cheshire Regiment as a Private soldier, number 45813. The young soldier may have been wounded or transferred due to battalion mergers. Consequently the Moreton soldier was transferred to the 1/S W Borderers where he received the number 41156.

On 19th October 1918 the battalion was involved in the capture of the village of Reget De Beaulieu, and the next day they tried in vain to capture machine gun nests. At dawn on the 21st the battalion HQ was heavily shelled, our artillery replying with 200 rounds. Later that day trench mortars, Lewis guns and rifle grenades engaged the machine gun positions. The battalion was relieved and moved back to comfortable billets at Wassigny (8 miles from Rethal, France).

On 22nd October the 1/SWB moved forward in support of the 2/Welsh Regiment who were attacking early next day. "D"

Company of the 1/SWB was attached to 2/Welsh Regiment under orders of the Officer commanding that battalion. On October 23rd at Zero, 01-20 hours the Welsh on left and the Gloucesters on the right attacked. The battalion was supporting the Welsh but was not required to take part in the action. The Bosche put down a very heavy barrage about two minutes after our barrage opened. "D" Company attached to the left attacking battalion had rather heavy casualties, sustaining 1 Officer dead, 5 other ranks wounded and a further 19 wounded. Amongst the dead was Private W A H Mercer.

The twenty year old soldier lies within grave reference XII A3, Highland Cemetery, Le Cateau, Nord France. The industrial town of Le Cateau, forever synonymous as the site of the Old Contemptibles initial engagement in 1914, lies 19 kilometres south east of Cambrai. Highland cemetery is about a kilometre south of the town on the D12 Road at Wassigny.

Throughout the war years the use of aircraft increased, technology extending the range and reliability of aircraft. While the Allies bombed Germany, this country also endured hostile raids, within their range being the industrial Midlands. However the raiders had now managed to bomb Liverpool, Crewe and Warrington. Although rather late in the day, in mid-November an Anti Aircraft detachment of the Royal Garrison Artillery relocated from Wallasey to Leasowe Common. This re-organisation of the Mersey Defences may have gone unrecorded except for an accident concerning Private Truesdale who broke his leg during the manoeuvre.

In the advance to victory a Moreton resident received a gallantry award, Corporal W M Douglas, 532505 of the 1/15 battalion of the London Regiment (Prince of Wales Own Civil Service Rifles) was awarded the Distinguished Conduct Medal. Corporal Douglas was thus honoured for conspicuous daring and initiative during the advance on Moniflains.

He made his way under heavy shell and machine gunfire and made contact with troops from another Division. He returned with detailed reports which did much to clear up ther situation; he continually carried messages under fire.

During the final stages of the war the fighting continued while German diplomats attempted to secure a satsifactory armistice.

The Germans were all too aware that since July they had lost almost 400,000 men who were now captives and over 6,300 field guns. By November the German nation was on the verge of revolution, the naval fleet at Keele mutinied, and disaffection rapidly spread to other parts. On November 8th the citizens of Munich rioted, followed by revolutionary riots throughout Germany. The national crisis precipitated the abdication of the Kaiser who fled to neutral Holland, as the might of the Central Powers dissolved. Bulgaria had capitulated first, followed by the collapse of Austria Hungaria, the surrender of German forces in East Africa rapidly followed.

In Europe the Allies continued to hammer away at the Germans and by 1st November British forces had reached the rivers Scheldt and Oise and captured Valenciennes. By 9th November the British Empire troops reached Tournai and advanced on Mons. On that same Saturday inside a railway carriage in an empty siding in the Forest of Compeigne German envoys attempted to broker an armistice. The Allies were in no mood for negotiation and dictated their stringent terms, much to the anguish of the assembled German emissaries. They were then faced with an ultimatum to decline or accept within seventy-two hours; during this period the fighting would continue. The envoys hastily departed to report to their superiors before returning and resuming talks on the eve of 11th November. At 5am on 11th November Germany reluctantly signed an uncompromising armistice with terms so severe that two decades later a humiliated Germany would again threaten the world. At the 11th hour of the 11th day of the 11th month of 1918 the fighting with Germany ended. Although the armistice required to be resigned every 30 days, the long awaited victory had finally arrived for Britain and her Allies. The peace treaty of Versailles, signed the following year, closed the curtain upon the Great War.

There was of course national celebrations throughout the victorious nations. However the public euphoria was attributed more to the ending of the holocaust, than to a great military victory. The four-year-long wait of attrition had cost Britain dearly, the butcher's bill being 723,000 dead and a further 1,500,000 maimed, wounded or disabled. The nation collectively mourned a lost generation, very few families emerged unscathed from the wholesale death and destruction. Peace brought its own set of problems to the government who were now faced with requests for the return of the mortal remains of the fallen, by families seeking re-interment of their loved ones in the local church yard. The practicalities of the task were impossible. Apart from the financial aspect, repatriation of servicemen until 1960 was against the law of the land, also thousands of servicemen had no known grave. Visitors to Parish cemeteries often assume they contain First War casualties, in the majority of instances this is incorrect. It is fairly common to see the details of a deceased serviceman, who died overseas etched on a family headstone and this serves more as a family's own private memorial than an indication of interment.

However, a high density of serviceman's graves can be the legacy of an auxilliary hospital. Numerous incumbants of Birkenhead's Flaybrick Cemetery originate from the now demolished St. James hospital, which was utilised as an auxilliary hospital during the Great War.

At Christ Church, Moreton a headstone bears testimony to the death of Lance Corporal James Heatley, regimental number 4792 of the KRR who died on 15th December 1918 at Laurentide Sanatorium, Montreal. He was the son of Ann and Andrew Heatley, two parents who appear to have been haunted by tragedy. Two of their teenage daughters were drowned off Leasowe Shore in 1905, followed by the death of a grandchild the following year; another daughter died three years later. Their son's death is not contained in the standard reference works of the Great War as he died after the armistice and his name is also omitted from the local memorials. The stone mason who etched the KRR on the headstone has omitted the letter C, thus it is assumed our Moreton soldier served with the Kings Royal Rifle Corps. He is interred in the soldiers plot, section 9, grave 933/K in the Mount Royal Cemetery, Montreal, Canada. Despite all efforts the author is unable to discover any further information concerning this man.

Trio of medals issued to a Great War veteran.

Left to right: 1914 star, British war medal, victory medal.

The next of kin of those who were killed in the conflict received the deceased's medal entitlement, an individually named commemorative plaque (Page 74), and a condolence letter on behalf of the king (See overleaf).

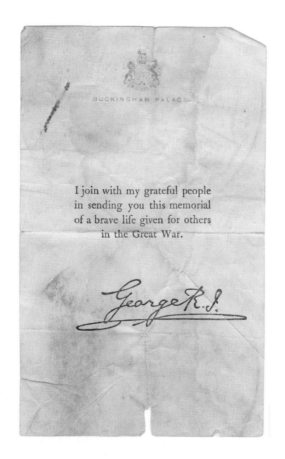

BUCKINGHAM PALACE

I join with my grateful people
in sending you this memorial
of a brave life given for others
in the Great War.

George R.I.

The arrival of the New Year heralded a new dawn and ushered in the first year of peace. Within weeks the Moreton villagers would again suffer the tragic death of one of their young men. There can be no harsher irony than to survive a war, only to be killed in peace time. It is possible that the young aviator witnessed the fund raising efforts for the Church roll of honour which later bore his name.

WILLIAM SMITH

LIEUTENANT   ROYAL AIR FORCE

William Smith was born on the 16th June 1899, the second son of Robert and Catherine Ann Smith. His father was a former Cammell Laird employee who established his own scrap metal company, from which he made a considerable fortune before his untimely death in 1909. The family home was originally "Holmlea", Glebe Road (now Glebelands Road); they later moved to "Cathcart", Hawthorne Road, which is now 8 Orchard Road, Moreton.

In late September 1914 William Smith volunteered. He was assigned to the Royal Army Medical Corps on 1st November 1914 where he served as a Private soldier. Amazingly the new recruit was only 15 years of age, and possibly one of the youngest soldiers on active service. Private Smith experienced all the horrors of the Gallipoli campaign and was wounded. He was invalided out of the Army on 30th March 1916; this may have been due to the Army realising his true age, as he appeared to have made a rapid recovery.

On 20 June 1916 he was employed as a Cadet by the Liverpool based Pacific Steam Navigation Company. At about this time he also served with the Royal Navy Reserve on HMS Delta and "Olympia". This was then followed by a transfer to the Royal Naval Air Service, which was then the naval wing of the Royal Flying Corps. The two arms of service were amalgamated in 1918 and became the Royal Air Force. On 5th August 1917 the Moreton youth gained his aviator's certificate number 7051. He was promoted to Temporary Probationary Flight Officer on 2nd June 1917 and a month later was posted to Manston Flying School, followed by RAF Branwell. A three month tour ended when he was brought home for service with the Grand Fleet. On 29 July 1918 he left Frinston to join the aircraft carrier HMS Furious, the 1916 built vessel being originally launched as a light battle cruiser. She underwent three flat top conversions before evolving into one of the earliest aircraft carriers. He served on "Furious" as an acting (Flying) 2/Lieutenant, before receiving promotion to Acting (Flying) Lieutenant on 1st April 1918, and four months later attained the rank of Acting (Flying) Captain. While still attached to "Furious" on 5th October 1918 he attended the fleet practice Station at Turnhouse, Firth of Forth. Captain Smith returned to his ship on Armistice Day.

During his war service the Moreton flyer flew the following aircraft, Maurice Farnam, Gnome, Avro V, Mono Avro, BeE 2c a two seater trainer and reconnaissance aircraft, also used as a light bomber. He also flew a single seater biplane fighter, the Sopwith Pup. The young aviator was anticipating an imminent promotion to Captain and a well-earned home leave of 28 days. He was now attached to HMS Valiant and was killed whilst on a flight to Scotland. His grave declares his date of death as the 29 January 1919, however the RAF state he drowned a day later. The cause of death was attributed to a manoeuvre known as "sideslipping". This is used by a Pilot to lose height with limited forward motion usually when landing, or to compensate drift just prior to landing. This is achieved by dipping one wing (or pair of wings) and allowing the aircraft to fall to that side. It appears that he was badly crushed by a collision and then met his death by drowning, possibly whilst attempting to land on the improvised carrier.

The drowned 19 year old aviator is interred in the family grave at Flaybrick Cemetery. This once impressive Victorian cemetery is now plagued by vandals, and sadly our young hero's grave has received the attention of the moronic element of today's society. As Lieutenant Smith died after the Armistice his death is not recorded in the standard reference works of the RAF. It is earnestly hoped this biography helps to redress the balance. Our intrepid hero who accomplished so much in his short life is commemorated on both local memorials.

The following illustration shows the type of aircraft used by Lt Smith landing on the ship upon which he served.

First aircraft to land on a ship underway was a Sopwith Pup, shown here landing on HMS Furious on 2nd August 1917

In order to perpetuate the memory of the men from Moreton and District who gave their lives in the Great War a meeting was held in the Assembly rooms one evening in mid-January. It was stated that 23 Moreton men had been killed in the war and between 90 and 100 servicemen returned to date. A committee was formed to open a subscription list to finance a memorial, the meeting was chaired by Rev W J Spinks, the Hon Treasurer being Mr W Briscoe.

At the beginning of February the Assembly Rooms was again the scene of a largely attended meeting of the inhabitants of Moreton, their purpose being to discuss what form the proposed memorial should take. The chair was occupied by Mr E Wilkinson supported by the Rev W J Spink and Rev R Powell of the Presbyterian Church. After much discussion it was unanimously decided that the proposed war memorial should take the form of a village hall in connection with the Church with proposed tennis courts and bowling green attached. As Moreton forms part of the Vyner family estate it was agreed the wealthy family should be approached for a grant of land for the memorial site. It was also decided to erect a memorial tablet within Christ Church with the names of the fallen on it, and in the Presbyterian Church a tablet of thanksgiving for the safe return of all servicemen members. The estimated cost of the memorials was £1,000 of which £200 had already been raised.

TO 27418 Private T W CLARKE

1st Garrison Battalion the Cheshire Regiment.

At last the time has come for you to return home. I cannot let you leave Gibraltar without thanking you for the part you have borne in the greatest war that has ever been fought in the cause of justice, honour, and a clean world for its children to live in. There can be no doubt the nation appreciates that it is due to the glorious spirit of patriotism and devotion to duty which has characterised each member of the Army in all parts of the world, that our great empire, instead of being vanquished, is to-day not only victorious, but greater then ever.

I trust your home-coming may be of the happiest and that you may have no difficulty in obtaining employment. I am afraid, though, you are sure to find a good deal of unrest in the labour world and would ask you to remember that peace is not yet signed, and that unless we are able to maintain the fine spirit of unity which has been such a marked feature in winning the war, we may find ourselves driven to make terms of peace which will not ensure the future of the world, for which you have been fighting.

If you are ever invited to join in a strike I implore you to hesitate, remembering that the Government and the People of England are determined to bring about a vastly improved standard of life for the Working Classes, and that any requests represented through the proper channels will be sympathetically considered, whereas disorderly strikes will not only play into the hands of the enemy, but will postpone the time when prices of necessities will fall and you can settle in your homes in peace and plenty.
I hope to say "Farewell" and "Godspeed" on board the Transport, ere the ship sails.

General, Governor and Commander in Chief.
Gibraltar.

18th February, 1919

Courtesy of Mrs. V. Beecroft

144

The military were slow to release the servicemen many of whom were increasingly anxious about their civilian job prospects. In fact thousands returned to mass unemployment and means tests of the great 1920s depression. In the Spring of 1919 no less than 63 Moreton personnel were still retained by the armed forces, while 90 demobbed soldiers had returned to village life.

On June 3rd George Cockerill, a timber merchant, and Silvester S. Morris, licensee of the Coach and Horses, in their capacity of Christ Church wardens and Rev. Spink gave permission for a stone memorial to be erected as a record and memorial of the men connected with the said church who fell during the recent war. It was, of course, a period when memorials were appearing everywhere, some of the monuments were war time souvenirs. Amongst the assortment of ordnance appearing throughout the Borough, the Central Square railway station at Birkenhead displayed two field guns, while Hamilton Square also had a field gun and a suggestion was made to accompany the gun with a particular tank. The "Birkenhead" tank which had been in the thick of the March retreat was lastly used for training purposes, its successor "Birkenhead II" was in action at St Quentin in September 1918, and having reached its objective it was ditched in enemy lines. It appears this suggestion was not taken up although West Kirby did in fact have a tank. The iron mastodon arrived by rail at West Kirby station, and made its penultimate short journey to Westborne Park, upon arrival the engines roared for the final time as it climbed the plinth of the old bandstand, after which the tank's engines were removed.

Every opportunity to swell the coffers of the Moreton War Memorial Fund was utilised. In mid-June a successful garden party to augment the memorial fund was attended by 150 guests, the genteel event being officially opened by Mr Briscoe. The activities included croquet, clock golf and tennis, and for the young at heart, Hoop-la, Coconut shies and a pipe stall, while a lady palmist proved to be very popular. Afternoon tea on the lawn was handed around by a number of the ladies. During the afternoon a gold wristlet watch (presented by Mrs George Cockerill) for which tickets had been sold for some time was drawn, the lucky winner being a soldier from Cork. In the evening a musical programme was given, the artists being Miss Toumey, and Messrs Stephenson, Toumey, Hayes and Kenny. The day's proceedings raised approximately £25.

It is assumed all the Moreton servicemen had returned safely from the armed forces by Sunday 6th July, when a united thanksgiving service was held at Christ Church. Due to the large attendance the 3 pm united service was held in the church yard, with an additional service at 6.30 pm. The following month the servicemen enjoyed a dinner and concert in their honour.

On 19 July at Whitehall a peace procession was held, but not to be outdone Moreton held its own Saturday afternoon celebration of Victory, all the proceeds again being donated to the War Memorial Fund. The usual hoards of summertime day trippers swelled the numbers attending the Victory Gala and Sports Event. Strings of flags were stretched across the fields and lanes with huge Union Jacks at strategic intervals, under which passed a procession. At the head was a carriage decorated to represent peace, followed by a beautifully decorated cart, with a number of children dressed in costumes representing the Allies, another cart with a tableau depicting haymakers, was followed by a fancy dress parade. As the procession entered the sports field the Albert Memorial Band struck up the National Anthem. The field contained several large marquees, surrounded by all the fun of the fair, including a boxing exhibition. Several hundred children also participated in various forms of races. During the afternoon excellent entertainment was provided under the direction of Mesdames Owen and Wilkinson with contributions from Mrs W B Owen, Mrs Wilkinson, Miss D Saltmarch, Messrs C Bibby, C Howden, A Bibby and H M Potter. The successful day of events culminated in an evening concert.

A further public meeting held in late August regarding the selection and purchasing by the committee of a memorial tablet revealed the fund now stood at £1,000. Although this figure appears to have met their original target, the fund closing date was now extended by six months. It was anticipated that various forms of entertainment taking place over the winter months would double the fund.

Sergeant Biddle returned safely from the war on 14th August but within four weeks he was involved in an accident reported by the local press thus. A nasty accident took place at Moreton when a motor car and motor cycle collided at the village cross roads. A young man named Percy Biddle and a friend Bostock both residing in the locality were on the motor cycle and the car was travelling from Birkenhead. The impact was a severe one, Biddle was thrown over the bonnet of the car and rendered unconscious, receiving nasty cuts and being badly knocked about. The motor cycle was badly damaged.

Private Joseph Clarke enlisted into the Kings Regiment in 1917. He completed training too late to see action, although be did serve after the war with the Rhine Army of Occupation. Under the terms of the Armistice German territory west of the Rhine, together with bridge heads, would be occupied for 15 years.

Photograph courtesy of Mrs V Beecroft

Private J Clarke depicted as a mounted soldier serving in the transport lines of the Kings Liverpool Regiment. In the right of the background the building appears to be a German style villa.

Photograph courtesy of Mr. L. Mitchell

The local press seemed to have ignored the efforts of the Women's War Memorial Committee which divided the Parish up into districts, to which a collector was assigned. An undated handwritten account in the Christ Church vestry diary records the collectors name and the designated addresses to cover were:-

Mrs Scott -
Stamford Road and Dial Terrace

Miss Hoey and Miss Gunh (writing indecipherable) -
Silverburn Avenue

Mrs Kenny -
Sunnyside, Pasture Road, Foreshore and Main Road, Leasowe

Mrs Symington -
Glebe Road

Mrs Wilkinson -
Main Road (Stores) and Digg Lane

Mrs White -
Moreton Terrace and Sandbrook Lane Shop

Mrs O'Donoghue -
Hawthorne Road and Park Road

Mrs Cockerill -
Church Road (Chadwick Street)

Miss Hale & Waring -
Saughall Massie

Due to illness Miss Spink took the place of the canvasser for Glebe Road.

A tea tent for holiday makers was again used to raise funds.

All the community's efforts were rewarded when a United service was held on the final Thursday evening of September at Christ Church, the occasion being the dedication of a handsome memorial tablet by the Arch Deacon of Chester "in grateful remembrance of the men from the parish who had served their King and Country in the Great War, especially those (25 in number) who had sacrificed their lives". The service was conducted by the Rector, Rev W J Spink, and members of the Presbyterian Church swelled the large congregation.

The Arch Deacon preached an eloquent and inspiring sermon and the "Last Post" was sounded at the conclusion of the service. The Memorial Hall which stands in Barnston Lane was erected in the Autumn of 1919.

NEWTON PRICE

PRIVATE 64576 3(RESERVE)
LANCASHIRE FUSILIERS

Nestling amongst the weathered memorials at Christ Church, Moreton stands the family grave of the Price family, the headstone also records the death of Private Newton Price, of the Lancashire Fusiliers. The engraving on the headstone is especially significant as it is the only known public record of this individual's service with the colours. His name is not included in the HMSO publication "Soldiers died in the Great War", nor does he appear on either of the village memorials. Eight decades after his demise the mystery was why not.

The mother of Newton Price was Emma Price who resided at 47 Lucerne Road, Seacombe. She passed away on 23rd April 1913 aged 36, and was interred at Christ Church. The deceased's sons and daughters may have been taken in by their Moreton relations. Their grandmother who had died the previous year had lived at Vandal Cottage, facing Moreton Common. At the time of his mother's death Newton Price would have been thirteen years old.

The young man was employed as a labourer at Merseyside Cake Mills and resided at Gorse Lane (now Burnley Road) Moreton. It is unknown whether Newton Price was an under age volunteer, but at the age of eighteen the young man would have been conscripted to the Army. Although the guns were now silent along the Western Front men were still required primarily for the Army of the Rhine. Private Price was assigned to the 3rd (Reserve) battalion of the Lancashire Fusiliers, who were based on the coastal peninsula at Withernsea. The battalion formed part of the Humber Garrison defending the vital ports of Hull and Grimsby. By now the reader will be accustomed to the tragic loss of young lives, and like the author they will doubtless be sad to discover the fate of this young man. The West Cheshire Coroner held an inquiry into the death of 19 year old Newton Price, after the deceased was found hanging in a caravan in Gorse Grove, Moreton. Recording a verdict of suicide, he added there was no evidence to show the state of this young man's mind at the time. This is truly the saddest of all biographies and is included only for the sake of historical accuracy. The former soldier who died on 8th October 1919 was interred in the family grave, reference East 496 on 13th October 1919.

In 1955 the Imperial War Graves Commission agreed to pay the Parochial Church Council (PCC) the sum of five shillings (25p) per annum to maintain the war grave of Newton Price, which was no longer maintained by relatives. The contract required the PCC to provide the following services:
a)   The keeping of the war grave clear of all weeds, stones, loose soil, rubbish, the mowing of grass from time to time as occasion requires, the filling up, levelling and returfing of all holes and bare places in the turf.
b)   The washing of the commission headstone as and when necessary but not less than once in each year by scrubbing with a brush and clean water only. In 1951 the PCC objected to this particular condition and sought an enhanced remuneration, the outcome remains hidden in the archives somewhere.

If the authorities were slow to release the servicemen, they were positively lethargic when it came to the repatriation of the prisoners of war. The German captives at Bidston began to react against their prolonged incarceration, much to the distress of the Moreton farmers. Increasingly reluctant to work the land the prisoners withdrew their co-operation, generally lounging about and refusing to work. During one such protest a wooden hut was set alight, the flames fanned across a neighbouring field resulting in the destruction of a crop of clover. This incident proved too much for the exasperated local farmers who were paying for the services of the prisoners. The Agricultural Executive Committee hired out the prisoners for a standard rate, based on the area's average wage for agricultural workers, and in turn the prisoner received a wage of 2d if acting as an NCO, 1.5d as a skilled worker or 1d if an ordinary worker. The average day's work was 8.5 hours with double time for overtime, the record for overtime was held by two prisoners in Yorkshire who worked 97 hours overtime. The prisoners began to be repatriated in September, and all the camps were reported as closed by the end of November.

The following is considered to be the only surviving record of Moreton, Leasowe and Saughall Massie First World War veterans. The majority of the information has been collated from numerous local history archives, news reports, etc. Naturally a few names could possibly be missing from the listing, as not all the records have survived. The Roll of Honour contains the names of 128 individuals which was considered to be a great patriotic response from the locality.

Typical details below record the names, rank, numbers, arm of service and place of residence in 1918.
* Denotes known brothers.

Moreton, Saughall Massie and Leasowe Roll of Honour for the Great War for Civilisation

ALLANSON, Francis Lawler.
Sgt. 355656. 10/Kings Liverpool Sandbrook House

AUSTIN, Richard.
Pte. 1/8 Lancashire Fusiliers Leasowe Lighthouse

BADDELEY, Thomas Gibson.
Pte. 676349. 285th Brigade Hawthorne Road

BAIRD, Andrew Graham.
Engineer. Royal Naval Reserve Died 1/8/17

BARCLAY, Eric Calandar*
Lt. Mech. Machine Gun Service KIA. 25/9/15

BARCLAY, William Keith*
Cpl. 66 Brigade Lancashire. 19/Kings Own Hawthorne Road

BEDE, George Templeton*
HMS Andes

BEDE, James Colin*
Pte. 270777. Royal Engineers Leasowe Embankment

BIDDLE, Edmund Glover*
Pte. T/220295 Army Service Corp Mech Transport.

BIDDLE, John Percival*
Sgt. 200430. 1/4 Cheshire Regiment Bankfield House

BLAKE, Harold
Cpl. 326387. IW & D Royal Engineers Stamford Road

BORROWMAN, Roy
Pte. 20197. 1/Kings Own Scottish Borderers Died 7/12/15

BOWMAN, Andrew
Pte. 17/Kings Liverpools KIA 29/4/18

BRISCOE, Harold
Denbighshire Yeomanry.

BROOKFIELD, Arthur Slade
Sgt 9023. 3/Cheshire Regiment Stamford Road

BROSTER, Edmund*
Pte. 4599. Cheshire Regiment Saughall Massie

BROSTER, Joseph*
Gunner. 77003. Royal Garrison Artillery Saughall Massie

CLARK, Thomas William
Pte. 27418. 1/Garrison Cheshires Moreton Terrace

CLARKE, Fredrick Sumner
Lt. 10/Kings Liverpool KIA. 14/10/18

COOPER, John
Pte. 11/Cheshire Regiment Wounded and gassed

COTTERELL, William Percy
Pte. 64737. 3/Cheshire Regiment 14 Silverburn Ave

DAVIES, Edward
R/Man 9/Kings Royal Rifle Corps DOW. 25/9/15

DAVIES, George Richard Weston (DCM)
Pte. 202524 Cheshire Regiment

DAVIES, Joseph
Pte. 303910 Motor Transport Dial Terrace

DODD, Henry
Cpl Royal Engineers

DOUGLAS, W M (DCM)
Cpl. 532505 1/15 London Regiment

DOYLE, Norman Dennis
Pte 1/5 Gordon Highlanders

DUCKERS, John
Cheshire Regiment and Machine Gun Corps

DUNCAN, William
11/Cheshire Regiment 5 Moreton Terrace

EASDOWN, Herbert
L/Cpl Cheshire Regiment

ENNION, George Edwin
Pte. 8/South Lancashires DOW. 28/4/18

EVANS, George Alfred
M/Shn HMS North Star

EVANS, Joseph
Pte. 2/South Lancashires KIA. 13/4/18

FENLON, John William
Sgt. Denbighshire Yeomanry Smithy Lane

FRENCH, John William
Pte. Royal Welsh Fusiliers KIA. 22/4/18

GEORGE, John B G
10/Kings Liverpool Leasowe Station Masters House

GREENWOOD, Charles Robert
PTE. 128388. 3rd Trainery Batt. Royal Army Medical Corps
Silverburn Ave

HALE, Robert
Kings Own Scottish Borderers

HARDCASTLE, Ernest*
Pte. G/16345. 9/Cheshire Regiment DOW. 16/9/16

HARDCASTLE, Thomas*
Pte. 11/Cheshire Regiment

HARDCASTLE, Oswald W
Sgt. 24031 13/Cheshire Regiment

HOWARTH, Crispin George
Cpl Royal Engineers

HUGHES, James
Pte 13/Cheshire Regiment Armchair Cottage, Hoylake Road

HUTCHINGS, Alfred John
Pte Royal Army Medical Corp

JOHNSON, William Lovelady
Pte. 31708. 1/Garrison Batt. Manchester Regiment

JONES, Alfred*
Pte. 1/Royal Welsh Fusiliers Stamford Road

JONES, David

JONES, John Henry*
Stamford Road

JORDAN, William
Pte. 51st Kings Loyal Regiment

KEENAN, Charles
Pte. 218995. Remount Dept. Army Service Corp Shirehampton,
Bristol. Glebe Road

KENTISH, George
Lieut Labour Infantry

KNOWLES, William Ernest
Royal Welsh Fusiliers Birkenhead Road

LATHOM, Adrian Percy
Cpl. 10/kings Liverpool. KIA. 21/9/18

LESTER, Edward
Pte. 11033. Royal Air Force Saughall Massie
Village

LESTER, J
Cpl 1/Cheshire Regiment

LINFIELD, Francis*
Wounded August 1917

LINDFIELD, Harold

LINDFIELD, William

LINFIELD, Percy*
11/Cheshire Regiment Digg Lane

LOVENE, Albert

LYON, Richard
Pte. 197001. Army Service Corps Supply Sunnyside

MADDOCK, Cyril Edward
L/Cpl Royal Welsh Fusiliers

MARTIN, Thomas Percy
Pte Army Medical Corps

MASON, Frank
Resided Vandal Cottage

MASON, Joseph Allen
Cpl Army Service Corps

MASON, Percy
Pte Royal Marines

MASON, Robert Henry
Royal Field Artillery

MASSEY, Louis* AB
Seaman. HMS Berwick & Submarine E53

MASSEY, Sydney*
1/Cheshire Regiment

MASSEY, Walter*
Pte. 7049. 1/Cheshire Regiment KIA 24/8/14

MEADOWS, William
2/Lt Northumberland Fusiliers Withom Farm

MEATES, John Lionel
2/Lt No 3 Coy. Army Service Corps Glebe Road

MERCER, W A Herbert
1/South Wales Borderers KIA. 23/10/18

MOORE, John
Pte. 2310 Army Service Corps Remounts 24 Stamford Road

MUTCH, Eric (DCM)
CS Major. 16340 Cheshire Regiment Smithy Lane

MUTCH, John

OWEN, Robert William Bertram
Lt Royal Anglesey Hawthorne Road

OWENS, Thomas
Pte. 355616 No 4 Coy. Army Service Corps

PARKINSON, George
Pte Royal Welsh Fusiliers KIA 12/11/16

PICKLES, James Fairhaven.
Hawthorne Road

PIPE, John Leslie Marconi
Officer HMS Transport

POSTON, Cyril Douglas
Sub/Lt HMS Heysham

POTTER, Francis
Sgt Cheshire Regiment

POTTER, Harold

POTTER, Henry
Pte. 50467 15/Cheshire Regiment Pasture Road

PRESTON, George Francis
Pte South Lancashire Regiment

PRESTON, Stanley
Pte Kings Liverpool Regiment

PRICE, Newton
Pte 3/Lancashire Fusiliers Died 8/10/19

RUDKIN, Thomas Charles
Pte Army Service Corps

RUTLEDGE, William Henry
Pte Royal Garrison Artillery

SMITH, Arthur Edward
86 CSMI. AGS War Hospital

SMITH, Edwin James
Pte Royal Engineers

SMITH, George
Sapper Royal Engineers

SMITH, Herbert Gardner
Pte 13/Cheshire Regiment DOW. 16/5/16

SMITH, Joseph
Main Road

SMITH, Percy
Pte. 11/Cheshire Regiment DOW. 13/10/16

SMITH,
Captain Navy Orchard Road

SMITH, William
Army Service Corps

SMITH, William
Lieut Royal Air Force Died 29/1/19

STANLEY, Arthur*
Drummer 11/Cheshire Regiment

STANLEY, Daniel*
Pte. 24461 11/Cheshire Regiment KIA. 7/6/17

STANLEY, Fredrick
11/Cheshire Regiment

STANLEY, John*
11/Cheshire Regiment

STANLEY, Norman
Pte Royal Engineers

STANLEY, Thomas*
Cheshire Regiment

STANLEY, William*
Dvr. Royal Horse Artillery, later Pte. 57100 1/4 Cheshires

SUTTON, Joseph
Sgt. 24472 11/Cheshire Regiment KIA. 10/4/18

TARRANT, James*
Pte. 206905 Motor Transport Birkenhead Road

TARRANT, William*

THOMAS, Frederick
11/Cheshire Regiment Stanford Road

THOMAS, Lawrence
Pte Army Service Corps

VAUGHAN, John Edward
Pte Royal Engineers

WARING, Thomas H
L/Cpl. 7/Kings Own Scottish Borderers KIA. 11/5/16

WARR, Frederick Francis
Pte City of London Cavalry

WARTON, Arthur Herbert
Pte Cheshire Yeomanry

WARTON, James
Pte Cheshire Regiment

WATLING, A Ernest
Cpl 1/Cheshire Regiment

WATLING, John*
Knutsford Road

WATLING, Harold*

WELSH, Ernest
325036 Dvr Royal Engineers BSB 5 Stamford Road

WESTON, Richard
S/363782 Pte Mersey Defence Army Service Corp

WILCOX, Ernest

WILKINSON, Reginald
Sgt 7/Reserve London Regiment

WILSON, Alexander M**
Pte South African Regiment KIA 14/7/16

WILSON, Henry*
Pte 1/4 Cheshire Regiment DOW 31/7/16

WILSON, J*
Pte Loyal North Lancashire Regiment Stamford Road

WILSON, W Denis**
Pte 10/Kings Liverpool Regiment KIA. 16/6/15

WRIGHT, HB (MC)
2/Lt. Cheshire Regiment. Late Denbighshire Hussars
3 or 8 Siverburn Avenue

Their name liveth for evermore

1920

The castle at Leasowe frequently mentioned in this tale again featured in a drama, this time in mid-January. No longer utilised by the military the now vacated premises were in the throes of a conversion to a convalescent home for railway men. At 2.00pm on Wednesday morning a fire broke out, the alarm was raised by a watchman whose prompt call out of the Wallasey Fire Brigade saved damage. During its use as a POW Camp the furniture was stored in the Star Chamber, which is beautifully panelled in black oak. The fire broke out in the rooms above and crept down the panelled wall to the room below, causing £50 worth of damage.

With the church memorial now complete the villagers now concentrated on the financing of the proposed memorial hall.

Towards the end of January on Thursday and Friday evenings an entertainment was given at the Presbyterian Church, Moreton in aid of the fund. Various sketches and tabloids were skilfully given followed by the children who staged a production of Little Red Riding Hood. Great praise was also expressed at the wonderful prescenium (arch or framework around a stage supporting the curtain) designed, built and presented by a Moreton resident. A cheque for the memorial fund was received by the Pastor, the Rev R L Powell. On Friday the fund received donations from Mr Clark and Mr T Harris, both of whom resided in Liverpool. The two evenings raised approximately £20 towards the fund.

Victory Hall

The parishioners were concerned about the health of the benevolent Rev Spinks, a man who appears to have been the lynch pin of the Moreton community. In late April it was announced that while he had not left the Royal Southern Hospital after his recent operation he was showing signs of a steady improvement.

The body count of the Great War continued to climb as the war wounded succumbed to their injuries, these men were often interred in public graves. The Government grant of £7-10s (£7.50) was inadequate for funeral expenses when a coffin alone cost £13. At this time a decent burial cost about £37-10s

(£37.50). One soldier however received a funeral worthy of a King, and while the odds are probably about the same as winning the National Lottery there is a remote chance he might have been a Moreton Patriot, such is the mystique of the "Unknown Soldier".

In the utmost secrecy four soldiers known only to God were exhumed from the Western Front, one of whom was selected by a blind folded Brigadier, to be the unknown soldier, his three anonymous comrades were quietly re-interred. The coffin bearing this unknown warrior was ceremoniously escorted across France, 35,000 French troops lined the route, school children were given the day off and the honour guard was led by wounded French veterans. From Boulogne the coffin and barrels of earth returned to Britain onboard the French warship Verdun. The cortege of the Unknown Soldier duly arrived at Victoria Station, from where it was ceremoniously escorted through the London throughfares. The route was lined by crowds with heads bowed in silent reverence, many of these observers may have contemplated that the remains of their missing son or husband was being conveyed upon the gun carriage. The coffin draped with a torn union flag from the battlefields solemnly trundled to Westminister Abbey via the new national war memorial. The temporary national war memorial erected in Whitehall for the peace procession of 19th July 1919 had been replaced. A new memorial had been commissioned to a design simplistic and purposely not of a triumphant nature. The monument sited in the heart of the capital became known as the Cenotaph, being a Greek word for an empty tomb. The Cenotaph was completed by Armistice Day 1920, and on this momentous day the Whitehall Cenotaph was unveiled by King George and the Unknown Warrior was interred.

The funeral cortege continued towards the Abbey, bordering the crowds was an honour guard of soldiers with their rifles reversed in silent salute, amongst their number being 100 holders of the Victoria Cross. In the presence of 2 Kings and 4 Queens, the Unknown Warrior was laid to rest within Westminister Abbey. The coffin which was made from a tree hewn from the grounds of Hampton Court Palace was bound with iron bands through which was inserted a Crusader's sword from the Tower of London. The casket was laid to rest upon the barrels of earth removed from the Ypres salient. By the end of the day the Centotaph was shrouded by wreaths and 20,000 solemn visitors had silently shuffled past the Westminister tomb. By the end of the month 1.5 million pilgrims had paid their respects to the Unknown Warrior.

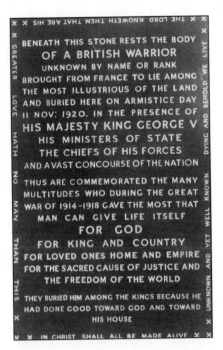

THE LORD KNOWETH THEM THAT ARE HIS

BENEATH THIS STONE RESTS THE BODY
OF A BRITISH WARRIOR
UNKNOWN BY NAME OR RANK
BROUGHT FROM FRANCE TO LIE AMONG
THE MOST ILLUSTRIOUS OF THE LAND
AND BURIED HERE ON ARMISTICE DAY
11 NOV: 1920. IN THE PRESENCE OF
HIS MAJESTY KING GEORGE V
HIS MINISTERS OF STATE
THE CHIEFS OF HIS FORCES
AND A VAST CONCOURSE OF THE NATION

THUS ARE COMMEMORATED THE MANY
MULTITUDES WHO DURING THE GREAT
WAR OF 1914-1918 GAVE THE MOST THAT
MAN CAN GIVE LIFE ITSELF
FOR GOD
FOR KING AND COUNTRY
FOR LOVED ONES HOME AND EMPIRE
FOR THE SACRED CAUSE OF JUSTICE AND
THE FREEDOM OF THE WORLD

THEY BURIED HIM AMONG THE KINGS BECAUSE HE
HAD DONE GOOD TOWARD GOD AND TOWARD
HIS HOUSE

IN CHRIST SHALL ALL BE MADE ALIVE

In an era when homes were devoid of wireless, and television was yet to be invented, the Cinema offered the public throughout the Kingdom a chance to see the Westminister ceremony. The Collins Picture Palace of Virginia Road, New Brighton secured the full local rights to show the ceremony. One week after the event the interment was shown in conjunction with the French war film "J'accuse". The following year a slab of Belgian marble was placed above the tomb, the inscription was inlaid from brass shell cases melted down after the war.

1922

With the turmoil of the war years now behind them, life for the majority of the nation returned to normal, the exception being the wounded servicemen who received little official recognition of their plight. Indeed the wounded and maimed were often ignored. Limbless, blinded and maimed ex-servicemen stoically endured financial and physical hardships in an era before the Welfare State. The Poppy Appeal and the Royal British Legion were conceived in an attempt to reduce the austerity imposed on the war widows, war wounded and former service personnel. Branches of the British Legion were soon established throughout the country, and on 29th March 1922 the Moreton branch of the Legion was formed, with a 161 strong membership. The second general meeting of the Moreton branch of the Legion occurred in early October in their newly acquired headquarters, the Moreton assembly rooms. In celebration of their new premises a whist drive and dance was held, during which the premises were officially opened. The branch also organised a Poppy Day collection in Moreton and District the lady collectors raised £40-10s-6d (£40.52p). On Armistice Day over 100 ex-servicemen attended church parade, before marching to the church to the martial strains of "The Boys from the Old Brigade", a wreath was placed at the Christ Church memorial tablet prior to the service.

1925

In November the Rev Spink acting as Hon Secretary to the Victory Hall informed the Committee of the Council's requirement for a portion of the Victory Hall's land in conjunction with the widening of Station (Pasture) Road. An agreement was reached with the Council who accepted the gift of the required land on the proviso they would reinstate the existing boundary wall and gateway. The Council Surveyor estimated the cost of work would be £72-16-10 (72.84p). The Victory Hall which was financed from the balance of the Christ Church memorial fund, now stands forlornly at the rear of the Moreton branch of the British Legion. The hall barred and locked when not in use by the St Johns Ambulance Brigade, shows no outer signs of its purpose as a memorial to the Moreton and District fallen of the Great War.

The Census returns for 1921 state the population of Moreton stood at almost 4,000, a figure which was seasonally boosted by 2,000,000 visitors per annum. To these visitors and new residents the village may have appeared devoid of a war memorial, a very easy misconception dependent upon your choice of religion.

1926

In this year the Moreton branch of the British Legion transferred their headquarters to a new site, the land adjacent to Christ Church which was purchased from a Mr Stern. In response to the Legionnaires requests for their own roadside memorial, several former servicemen constructed a large memorial, the design of the memorial, flower beds and approaches being conceived by Mr Arthur Smith of the School House, Moreton. The memorial originally stood directly in front of the new Legion premises, and faced onto Upton Road. The 10th November 1926 edition of the Cheshire and Birkenhead Advertiser reported on Wirral's latest memorial as follows:

MORETON ARMISTICE SERVICES
A CALVARY CROSS UNVEILED

The most successful Armistice Memorial Service yet held in Moreton took place on Sunday last. Over 100 ex-servicemen paraded in the village at 9.30am, commanded by Major K Barclay, MC and after a short route march attended the Parish Church, where a special service was conducted. The Parish Council, Boy Scouts and members of the Womens Section British Legion also attended. The service commenced with the processional hymn, "*Onward Christian Soldiers*" and after special prayers had been recited, two legionnaires, one Naval and one Military, advanced to the chancel steps, took up a wreath which had been placed there, and hung it on the Memorial Tablet on the North wall of the church. After this a two minutes silence was observed "*in remembrance of those who make us better men and give us peace in our time*".

A bugler of the 4/5th Cheshire Regiment then sounded the "*Last Post*" and the "*Rouse*", which was followed by John S Arkwright's well known hymn "*O valiant hearts*". During the singing of this hymn Mr Wray, Chairman of the local branch of the British Legion, advanced to the altar rails with the Legion colour, which was received by the Rector, who laid it upon the Holy Table. At the completion of the hymn he dedicated the colour, "*In the faith of Jesus Christ we dedicate this flag to his glory and as a symbol of the organised service we are called to render to those for whom He suffered and died*". The colour was then returned to the bearer, who received it and retired.

At the conclusion of the prayers the hymn "*For all the saints*" and the anthem "*Give us peace in our time O Lord*", followed. The Rev R L Powell, minister of the Presbyterian Church, gave a short address from the chancel steps. He quoted Lawrence Binyon, "*They shall not grow old as we that are left grow old. Age shall not weary them, nor the pressing of years condemn them. At the going down of the sun, and in the morning we shall remember them*". He said that the service stood for two things, remembrance and re-dedication. We were not only to remember those who had gone out from the village, a mere fragment, but all those who gave their lives and were unknown to us. He remarked how little notice was taken of the memorial at the Pier Head by those who frequently visited Liverpool, and suggested that if anyone had to hurry for a train and found the gates still open we should reflect that those who had laid down their lives had opened to us the gates of freedom. We should also re-dedicate ourselves to the history of the past, to soldiers, sailors, martyrs, scientists, and medical men, who had died in agony for the benefit of mankind, and men like the engineers of the "*Titanic*", who kept their posts in darkness while the bandsmen played a most appropriate hymn tune.

At the conclusion of the service, the choir, clergy and Legionaries proceeded to the adjacent head-quarters, where Major E S Law, 59th (4th West Lancashire) Medium Brigade Royal Artillery, unveiled a memorial in the form of a Calvary Cross, with halo erected by an anonymous donor, "*To the Glory of God and in remembrance of those who died in the Great War*". The memorial when complete will bear the inscription "*In Remembrance 1914-19*", and the names of all those now on the mural tablet in the church. The Rector said a dedication prayer, and the bugle sounded again. A wreath was deposited at the plinth of the cross, two maimed ex-servicemen being selected for the purpose, J Trotter, Leading Stoker, Royal Navy and Private J Berry, 9/ Welch Regiment.

The Legion then formed column of route, headed by the Birkenhead Postal Band (Mr Harland, bandmaster) and marched to the Upton Memorial where a short service was conducted by Canon Bellamy, Legion chaplain.

In the evening a joint service was held in the Picture Palace, Mr Wray in the chair, the clergy present being the Revs, the Rector, Canon Bellamy, and Father Griffin. The Rev R L Powell sent a letter of apology for his absence owing to throat trouble, dangerous in the night air. Mr George Cockton presided at the piano, and Mr Tom Hurley was present with his cello. The opening was a voluntary "*Traumerie*" by Schumann, after which followed the hynm "*O God our help in ages past*", and after prayers by Canon Bellamy, followed by an address on the meaning of Armistice Sunday, leaving the actual day for jubilation.

The Rector spoke in praise of the local branch of the Legion, which had now reached a point deserving of all possible help,

Photograph courtesy of Mrs. Burrows

and he appealed to all ex-servicemen who had not joined to do so. Father Griffin expressed a hope for increased membership and greater local interest.

1927

In November a brass plaque inscribed with the names of the *"Moreton Patriots"* and their relevant regiment was added to the memorial. The cost of the plaque engraved by J Ball of Vernon Street Liverpool was £20, payable from the £23 raised from a public appeal. The balance of the fund contributed towards the transport costs of the Birkenhead Postal Band, the Moreton Armistice Service musicians.

After the end of the Second World War Moreton witnessed another expansion. This was principally due to a shortage of housing, property developers being attracted to Moreton where land was available at 7s 6d (37p) a square yard (approximately a metre). The increasing population also required churches, and in January 1950 the fund-raising for the new Sacred Heart Church was boosted by the Hollywood Star Bing Crosby who forwarded a donation of 25 dollars to buy 24 square yards of the Church's two acre site. The star who had been contacted by a parishioner had recently played a Catholic priest in the films *"Going my way"* and *"The Bells of St. Marys"*. In a letter to the then Father Rees it was stated the amount was from the royalties of his recordings of *Adeste Fideles* and *Holy Night*.

In the late forties concerns were expressed over the deterioration of the War Memorial and surrounding gardens, which were additionally spoiled by the erection of buildings close to the site. The Moreton branch of the British Legion which had recently opened new premises, urged Wallasey Town Council to provide a new memorial on a site in Pasture Road alongside the Victory Hall. The Legion maintained they should not be expected to finance the project, and as the Memorial was public property they considered it the Council's duty to finance the memorial; the Council shrewdly disagreed.

In September 1949 Mr Vyner, for a nominal sum, sold the field adjoining the Victory Hall to the Moreton branch of the Legion. The decision to move the Memorial to this site appears to have been instigated by Mr Jack Cross. Upon taking office as Chairman of the Moreton branch of the Legion he *"resolved to do something about the memorial before his year of office was over*". In an attempt to minimalise the project cost the field in which the Memorial was to be sited was cleared and levelled by Legion members.

The first physical attempt to move the Memorial was thwarted by the "*snapping of a crane*". Two days later, early on Monday morning 10th October 1949 the Memorial was moved from Upton Road to Pasture Road. The whole operation of lifting the cross and repositioning it was completed in just under an hour. The Memorial now in an elevated position at what was then the heart of the community was widely praised. The contract for the landscaping of the new site appears to have been awarded to HGB Construction Company of Moreton, their plans envisaging gardens, ornamental surrounds, rock gardens and a pair of wrought iron gates. For ease of maintenance the entrance gates were locked, and visitors to the Memorial obtained the key from the keeper of the Victory Hall. New houses were promptly erected on the vacated Legion site, the neat cul-de-sac was named Winston Grove, after Mr Winston Churchill.

On Sunday 6th November 1949 following a service at Christ Church the procession to the Memorial surrounded by the new Garden of Remembrance was led by the Salvation Army Band. The Legionnaires were headed by their standard bearer, Mr J Mercy, closely followed by the Womens Section standard bearer, Mrs Harrison and representatives of many local organisations. In the cold sunshine of a wet Autumn morning and with collars turned against the wind several hundred people gathered around the Memorial. At 11.00am heads were bared while two minutes silence was observed. The service opened with a dedication of

*Thiepval memorial to the missing of the
somme.*

*Ploegsteert memorial to the missing.
Photograph courtesy of the
commonwealth war graves commision.*

*Menin Gate, memorial to the missing of
the Ypres salient.*

the Memorial clean and bright on its new site by the Rev J Edwards, Rector of Moreton, the lesson was read by the Rev R E White, Moreton Baptist Minister. While the standards were slowly lowered "*The Last Post*" was sounded by Mr J K Povall, the minutes silence being ended by the exhortation given by Captain Brock. Reveille brought standards up to their full height and prayers were said by the Rev Arfon Price. Wreaths and flowers were then placed at the foot of the memorial, and the service which was the best attended for many years came to a close with the singing of the National Anthem.

Towards the end of November the Moreton branch of the British Legion launched an appeal for funds to defray the cost involved in the restoration of the Moreton War Memorial. The maintenance of the Memorial and the garden became the responsibility of the British Legion Moreton Branch which stated it would oversee that work would be carried out successfully, and the site maintained so that never again can it be said that our fallen comrades have been forgotten by us.

In 1949 the memorial did not bear the names of those killed in the Second World War, and for the memorial's dedication a sheet of card bearing approximately sixty names was affixed to the Memorial. The Moreton branch of the Legion appealed for the names of all the local men and women who fell in the recent war, so that a memorial plaque could be added. The new plaque bearing the following seventy-nine names of men and women was dedicated on Armistice Sunday 1950.

Moreton and Districts Patriots 1914-1919

J A ANKERS	A F ASKEW	A BARKER
T F BEARE	J H BEECROFT	J R BIRD
G BOOTH	J F BORROWS	E BRASSEY
J CANAVAN	E I CLASSON	GW CORKHILL
F CROWDER	J H DANTON	R DAVIES
L S DOLPHIN	W DUNBAR	D J ECKBERRY
W V ECKBERRY	F EDMONSON	F W EDWARDS
D EVANS	J EVANS	J FAIRFIELD
F FIRMIGAN	J FLANDERS	R GELDART
A L GORDON	S GRAVES	G T HALLET
T F HAYDEN	G E HIDE	J HOEY
T HUGHES	S J HUNT	K R INGER
E INKSTER	G K JOHNSON	J A JONES
T F JONES	V W JONES	C R KEAT
A H KEEN	A E KNOT	S F LILLIE
D W McCALLUM	R B McCOMBE	N D McEWAN
R MIDDLEBROOK	W MORAN	G MORRIS
R MORRIS	J MORTON	W PARKINSON
R C PARRY	A J PARSONS	R G M SHERLOCK
A SMITH	E E SMITH	H A SMITH
R S J SMITH	J SOAR	A SPEED
T H STOREY	J TABERNER	W G TARRANT
R TAYLOR	L THOMPSON	N TONER
E S TURNBULL	J E WALKER	R WALKER
J M WARLEY	J A WATERMAN	R B WHAMBY
J W WHITTLE	A WIGGINS	T A WILKINS
	S WILLIAMS	

In more recent times the name of E SPEAKMAN was added.

As the new millennium approaches, the monument continues to be maintained by the Moreton branch of the British Legion, the final alteration to the memorial consisting of short decorative railings around the memorial steps. On behalf of the community the author wishes to thank the members past and present of the Moreton British Legion for their efforts in lovingly maintaining the memorial.

Moreton and Districts Patriots 1914-1919

BIBLIOGRAPHY

Tennent A J. British merchant ships sunk by U-boat in the 1914-18 war. Starling Press (1990)

Laffin J. Damn the Dardenelles. Budding Books (1997)

McCarthy C. The Somme - the day to day account. Arms & Armour Press (1993)

Warner P. World War One, a narrative. Cassel Military Classics

Gamiln H. Twixt Mersey & Dee. Cedric Chivers Ltd (1992)

Hammerton Sir J A. A popular history of the Great War. Amalgamated Press

Hurst S C. The Silent Cities. Naval & Military Press (1994)

Coombs R. Before endeavours fade. Plaistow Press (1994)

James E A. British Regiments 1914-18. Naval & Military Press (1978)

Lys I. Delville Wood

McDonald L 1915 The Death of Innocence. Penguin (1993)

Simkins P. Chronicles of the Great War. Colour Direct (1997)

Soldiers died in the Great War 1914-19. His Majesty's Stationery Office (1921)

Officers died in the Great War 1914-19. His Majesty's Stationery Office (1919)

Sulley P. The 100 of Wirral. Cedric Chivers Ltd Bristol (1993)

Liverpool's Scroll of Fame. Quills, Liverpool (1920)

The Kings (Liverpool Regiment) 1914-19. Gale & Polden, Aldershot (1920)

Marquis de Rivigny Roll of Honour. Vol 2, p188

McGilchrist A M. The Liverpool Scottish 1900-19. Henry Young & Sons, Liverpool (1930)

Wyrall E. The History of the Kings (Liverpool) Regiment 1914-19 (three volumes).
Edward Arnold & Co (1928)

Acknowledgments to:

Commonwealth War Graves Commision

Merseyside Maritime Museum

Public Record Office

The following Regimental Museums, for providing the battalion information;

Kings Royal Rifle Corps, South Lancashires, Royal Welsh Fusiliers, South Wales Borderers, Liverpool Scottish.

All the families who have contributed to this project

My next project concerning the Great War will be the History of the 15th and 16th battalions of the Cheshire Regiment better known as the "Birkenhead Bantams". The members of these battalions, originally deemed unsuitable for military service due to a lack of height, proved their worth on the battlefields of France and Flanders. I would be extremely grateful for information or the loan of artefacts relating to these volunteers. Please contact the author at Wirral Rocking Horses, telephone 0151 606 1177 during business hours only.

Index